NO FIXED ABODE

CHARLIE CARROLL

A JOURNEY THROUGH HOMELESSNESS FROM CORNWALL TO LONDON

summersdale

ABOUT THE AUTHOR

Charlie Carroll is a writer, musician, teacher and traveller. He lives in Cornwall with his wife and their cat, Digby. His first book, *On the Edge*, combined travel writing with the exploration of social issues, namely the state of British education. It was described by the *Daily Mail* as 'A profoundly shocking book' and as an 'important read' by *The Times Educational Supplement*. Charlie has spoken on local BBC radio stations and BBC Radio 5Live, and written for *The Guardian* and *The Big Issue*. You can read more about Charlie's work at www.charliecarroll.co.uk and find him on Twitter at @CharlieCarroll1.

For my wife
Michelle

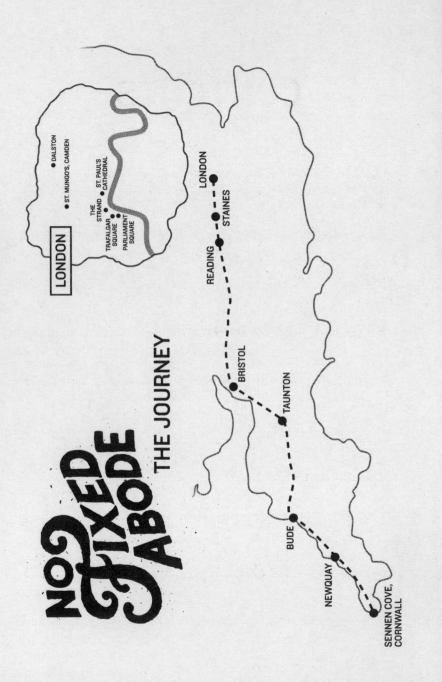

CONTENTS

CHAPTER ONE

PREAMBLE

I

Where should the book of a journey begin? Should it be in the car or the bus, above the tyres, en route to the train which in turn leads to the airplane or boat? Or should it be later, triggered by touchdown and passport control? Should the opening line depict the first sense of a different climate? Perhaps it should wait even longer, starting with familiarity and comfort rather than rampant ticket-searches, airport farewells, jet lag and acclimatisation. Because everything before that, they say, is just a preamble.

My journey began the moment I stepped out of my front door, locked it, and then pushed the keys back through the letterbox. My official starting point, a small beach called Sennen Cove, was an hour's bus ride away, or a day's walk. I started as I meant to go on, and strode down the hill. That morning, the news had been of the fire of riots which blazed its way from London to Birmingham: a montage of men dragged from their motorbikes, balaclavas and shattered shop windows, exhausted policemen asleep on tables, community clean-ups, flaming department stores and looters, looters, looters. If I was to become a tramp, now was an opportune time: more people than ever had taken to the streets.

2

The itch never started in my feet – instead, it manifested itself in sharp, fleeting prickles across my forehead, a slight twitch around the eyelids, and an increasing habit of spinning the globe hung from string above my desk and gawping soundlessly at the yellow and green patches of land which came to a stop before me. My wife sometimes caught me doing it, and she recognised the symptoms before I did. This wanderlust was a perennial fever, and it had not, as we had both expected, diminished as I shifted into my thirties.

The academic year was drawing to a close, governmental cuts had hit my school hard, and my temporary contract was not to be renewed. My previous travelling had been limited to the six-week summer holidays, and I had used them most years in East Asia and East Africa. This year, with no September return to the classroom, I had as much time as I wanted, but I did not have the money.

I considered various options: backpacking was cheap if you did it right, but the plane fares were too expensive to justify; teaching abroad would take me anywhere in the world and pay me for the privilege, but all contracts demanded at least one year, and I could not bear to be away from my wife for so long; a seasonal job on Alpine slopes could be nonchalantly dropped after a few months, but, at thirty-one, I was already too old for the epicurean nihilism which dictated the days and nights of those fresh-faced gap-year students who staffed the pistes, and who saw a hangover as a temporarily inconvenient half-hour the morning after.

Still, the urge persisted. In bed at night, I thumbed through old guidebooks for the Philippines, Kenya and Nepal, searching for the pencilled circles I had made on the maps, around hostel addresses and bus stations and bars, as cues for nostalgic reverie.

'Jesus, Charlie,' my wife, exasperated, finally declared. 'Just go for a bloody *walk*!'

An idea flashed, built, revolved and then set. I tentatively explained its outline to her.

'Sounds good to me.'

'So you wouldn't mind? It might take a few months.'

'If it'll stop you moping around the house like you've just had to put your dog down, you should do it.'

I loved my wife.

The idea was so simple it startled me. I had little money; I had much time: what better thing to do than walk? Cornwall's coast was not far from my house – perhaps I could walk the whole 630-mile South West Coastal Path from Exmoor to Poole? Even better, I could follow in the footsteps of one of my favourite travel writers, John Hillaby, on a reverse JOGLE from Land's End to John O'Groats. I had no tent, but I had a good sleeping bag bought for a winter in Tibet a few years before, a mini-stove and mess tins to cook with along the way, and I was strong enough, healthy enough and motivated enough to do it. I began to practise, ignoring my fuel-thirsty van whenever possible and walking to and from plotted destinations that stretched me a mile or two further every day. I learned that I could travel four miles an hour on a flat, and that I could walk for up to eight hours providing I rested once every two. I borrowed friends' dogs for the day to lend an excuse for long excursions across Bodmin Moor and along tributaries of the River Fal. The frequent exercise grew addictive, and I fancied that I could feel my legs strengthening and my heart rate slowing.

At home in the evenings, spreadeagled on the couch, I revisited old books I had not read for years: books about walking, books about England, and sometimes books about both. Iain Sinclair followed Laurie Lee, Paul Theroux followed John Hillaby, but always, between and above them all, came George Orwell. There was a theme in those early works of his – *Keep the Aspidistra Flying*, *A Clergyman's Daughter*, and, most crucially, *Down and Out in Paris and London* – which I could not dispel.

How about, I thought, *walking, but walking as a tramp*?

Did tramps even exist any more? I considered the idea of becoming one, a tramp in twenty-first-century England, walking the ley lines of the country, existing both for and by movement. The notion seemed educational but whimsical, romantic even, yet underneath it a viable darkness bubbled.

It would mean, I thought, *becoming homeless*.

3

I had never been homeless, but I had come close, or thought I had. For eighteen months, I had lived in a rusting, leaking

VW Camper van, sleeping for the most part in free lay-bys. Once, I found myself in York, Saturday-tripping through the Viking streets. I parked on the outskirts of the city. Five carefully arranged cardboard boxes had been crammed beneath a nearby stairwell, and three men sat amongst them. One nervously hopped over to me.

'Love your van, mate,' he said.

'Me, too,' I replied. 'She's done me proud.'

'Any chance you could spare a bit of change? Me and my brothers over there…' – he gestured to the cardboard boxes beneath the concrete overhang where his two companions crouched and stared at us – '… we wanna try and get into the local hostel tonight. It's gonna be a cold one.'

I did not doubt it. It was early February and, though only three o'clock in the afternoon, the bite of a winter's night was already in the air. 'I've got a few quid,' I said, taking out my wallet and handing him the coins.

'Thanks mate, thanks. Really appreciate it.'

'Listen,' I said. 'I'm going to brew a cup of tea. Why don't you grab your mates and join me? I've got enough.'

'Nah,' he replied, backing away. 'Good of you to offer, mate, but nah, we're all right.'

'I know what it's like,' I remonstrated. 'I've just spent the winter in this thing. It's freezing out there. Come and have a cup of tea.'

The man stopped walking and stared hard at me. I felt suddenly scared. 'Know what it's like?' he whispered. 'You ain't got a fucking clue, mate! See this here?' He smacked the side of the van with an open palm, sending several splinters of rust to shatter on the ground. 'This is fucking *luxury*, this is.

You think you're homeless just because you've spent winter in a van? Tell you what, spend the night with me and my brothers over there. We'll show you what fucking homeless is all about.' He lurched forward, as if about to strike me, then perhaps felt the coins embedded in his fist, for he uncurled his fingers and looked at them for a moment. 'Thanks for this though, mate,' he said, all traces of anger vanished. 'You have a good one, yeah?'

He was, of course, right. My eighteen months living in the van had been a far cry from genuine homelessness. To assume as much to this man was feeble, the play-acting of a soul trying to convince itself of its false nobility. I was not homeless and I never had been. I had slept rough, but it was a dabble: the promise of a bed and a hot meal always existed on the fringes of my experimentation, no matter how far I strayed from them.

In my late teens and early twenties, as a poor, aimless and happy backpacker in Europe, I had tinkered with sleeping rough as a kind of rite of passage or a test of my own endurance. Those odd nights on park benches in Florence and Thessaloniki had not come from desperation, but from will; the weekend I spent camped out in Geneva airport because I could not afford a hostel had been, to my nineteen-year-old self, remarkably fun; and the long night outside Istanbul train station had been precisely the same, though that was tempered somewhat when I awoke at three in the morning to find a grinning Turk spooning behind me, staring at the back of my head, and feverishly masturbating.

I once spent a week hitch-hiking down the Costa del Sol, getting drunk in strange bars in Fuengirola or Estepona or Puerto Banús with my backpack beneath my bar stool, stumbling down to the beach to fall asleep on a wooden sunlounger, and then waking with crusty eyes to a bright morning and a fat north-Englander saying: 'Have yer paid for this, lad? No? Well, she 'as, so get on.'

I was no stranger to the streets. At the age of sixteen, while my friends worked in shops, waited in cafes and cleaned in hotels each weekend, I made my spare change with my guitar, busking upon my home town's pedestrianised thoroughfares. The guitar came with me to Europe: it was my lofty idea to busk my way around the continent's cities. Chased off the pavements of Kalamata by the Greek Mafia, almost arrested on Prague's Charles Bridge for lacking a permit, my guitar strings cut with a penknife outside the Uffizi, and my songs drowned out by the blaring of didgeridoos on either side of me in Covent Garden, I finally found Las Ramblas in Barcelona. I lived there for two months, belting out acoustic songs under the torrid Spanish sun to the waves of passing tourists. The pesetas they dropped into my guitar case paid for my *bocadillos* each day and my San Miguels each night, but my accommodation – which outweighed the earnings of all but my best days – always came from my savings.

That was the crucial difference. For all my posturing, I had never *needed* the streets. I was poor, but I knew it, and I had worked hard at two jobs before leaving home so that, no matter how little I made busking, I could always rely on the ATM to set me up for another night with a bed. When the clock passed midnight and Las Ramblas got dangerous, I had a room waiting.

Nevertheless, I grew friendly with a few from the city's street-level subculture: the buskers from all over the world who kept their pitches at a respectful distance from each other and then drank away their earnings together at night, trading stories of busking hotspots across the globe; the gangs of boys at Plaza de Catalunya who skateboarded and smoked weed for ten hours a day because they had nothing else to do; the beggars who curled up along the alleyways of the Arab Quarter and who often spoke less Spanish than I did. I was tolerated because I was on the streets every day, and so were they, and recognition blossomed into nods into greetings into friendship.

There was, however, another group of street-dwellers, perhaps the most populous, and they were relentlessly unsociable, even to each other. My busking friends called them *Los Locos* – 'The Crazies'. Singular, solipsistic, cursed with a plethora of mental-health issues, they wafted through Barcelona like ghosts, lost in anxieties no one could explain.

One of *Los Locos* – an old Catalan lady who hissed at me like a cat whenever I asked her questions or offered her some of my spare change – policed the alleyway down which my *pensión* lay. She slept there each night on top of a mattress blackened with scum, which she had wedged beneath the right-angled overhang where two buildings met. She slept there for only a few hours each night: at dawn she would be gone to walk up and down Las Ramblas from the Plaza de Catalunya at the top to the Christopher Columbus statue at the bottom. Before her, she pushed a supermarket trolley which held her entire belongings encased in plastic carrier bags. From each corner of the trolley a broomstick poked up above the bags, a teddy bear anally impaled upon each. When she returned to her mattress late at night she would stand beside it with an empty plastic bottle in each hand, alternating between bashing them together in a flamenco rhythm, and then hurriedly shouting into the neck of one as if it was a microphone, and she a radio commentator.

Los Locos were impenetrable, but they were for the most part harmless, too enveloped in their own fear to foist it upon anybody else. But there was plenty of danger on the streets. By day, tourism ruled Las Ramblas; by night, it was reserved for crime. I was never beaten, but I saw it happen to too many others, sometimes with weapons, and it made me sick no matter how drunk I was. Once, I was mugged at four o'clock in the morning by six fifteen-year-olds. I nearly laughed, but then one grabbed my hand and placed a knife against my wrist. And I finally left Barcelona because of a threat – I had told two American girls that the Romanian gangs who played 'Find the Lady' along Las Ramblas were con-artists, had pointed out the stooges and the lookouts who kept watch for police, and warned them never to play. The girls had then marched over to the gang they had lost money to the day before and demanded their pesetas back: they knew it was all a hoax, they said, the long-haired British busker down the road had explained it to them. That afternoon, I was approached in a bar by a man with an Eastern European accent and a web of thin scars across his hands who told me I should leave. I took the next train to Malaga, which departed before darkness dropped.

Soon after that, I returned to England and got a job, and my time on the streets dwindled.

4

Putting myself back on the streets would be an act of decisive will; one which, I knew, few others who slept rough had the luxury of. Reading books, articles and web pages on homelessness before I embarked on my journey, it became clear that, for most, that first drop, the initial slip into homelessness, is rarely purposeful. Often, it comes from something uncontrollable: trauma, an accident, job loss, debt, addiction. Nobody chooses to be homeless, but some people do choose to be *house*less. In the long history of English popular culture, such people have been called tramps.

'Tramp' is a debatable term and, as we push deeper into the twenty-first century, it has grown increasingly pejorative. The public consciousness of anyone nomadic and unsettled has become peppered with distrust and scorn. The word 'gypsy' used to be double-edged: for some, it depicted baby-snatchers, thieves and tinkers, the source of the local curse which had caused last year's harvest to fail miserably; but for others a gypsy was the harmless itinerant in his ornate walnut-shell caravan, who tourists photographed and locals donated food to – Danny the Champion of the World. Now, it means only 'pikey'; it means hostility, illegal camping and shock-reality TV programmes, all colluding to paint the word 'gypsy' black and the word 'traveller' – once so harmless – even blacker.

'Tramp' has similar twenty-first-century connotations, and its etymological root, the verb 'to tramp', is now all but obsolete in favour of the downbeat noun. Yet tramps, like gypsies, also have a legitimate, and sometimes ameliorative, history. For many years, tramping was a lifestyle and, often, a purposeful one. From the Elizabethan to the Victorian ages, to go 'on the tramp' would be to use well-known paths and networks to travel from town to town in search of casual work. It was viable, it could even be respectable, and there was something exclusively English about it. The Americans have their bums and hobos romanticised by Kerouac and his Beats, with their bindles and brown paper bags, hopping between railroads and park benches; the Indians their ascetic sadhus with their ochre body paints and yogic incantations; the Germans and French their journeyman carpenters and smiths who completed their apprenticeships and became masters of their trade by wandering between villages and refining their crafts in workshops across the country; but the tramp with his long coat, his worn shoes, his beard, his tea and tobacco – he is necessarily English, as much a part of our island-culture and our definition of self as red postboxes, subtle irony and rain.

For some, the age-old urge to roam – to be nomadic – is deep, while in others it is non-existent. When my first book – *On the Edge*, about a previous journey of mine through England – was published, I received an email from a man who had been my best friend when I was eight years old, and who I had not heard from in over a decade. 'My wife bought me your book for Christmas,' he wrote. 'I recognised you in it instantly. I remember you once telling us you had cycled to the Tesco in Truro. That seemed to me a world away.'

He now lives less than a mile from the house he grew up in.

Another friend, as I was leaving to travel for the first time at the age of eighteen, asked me: 'Why are you going travelling? What else do you need?'

He still lives in his parents' house.

Where I come from, few people leave. When I did, some considered it traitorous.

Others, however, those who knew me best, saw it was inevitable. My heroes were Laurie Lee, Heinrich Harrer, Jack Kerouac, George Orwell, Bruce Chatwin, and I was youthful and fanciful and silly enough to see the romance of nomadism, the liberation of solo travel. Perhaps if I had been born a hundred years before, I would have been a tramp. Then, the stigma was milder.

But there are few tramps these days. It is wrong to think that they have evolved into the homeless. There has always been a homeless population in Britain, just as there has always been poverty, deprivation and ruin in Britain. Tramps have instead been translated. They are today's backpackers and travellers, temporary tramps, for whom nomadism is an itch scratched in youth. A tiny minority leave home and then never return, bouncing around the globe between Peru, Thailand, Kenya and Greece until only the calcification of old age can halt their movement. But most come back, come back home, where the itch either heals or is repressed, surfacing at those times when nostalgic rumination allows it.

Orwell would have disagreed with me. The tramps he knew did not move because they were in essence nomadic; they moved because they had to, for the spikes in which they slept each night would not accommodate them more than once a month. Tramps tramped because there was nothing else they could do. And, as for deliberately taking to the road, Orwell could not even conceive of this – no Englishman, he believed, would embrace poverty on purpose. Tramps did not choose unemployment: they either could not find work, or had to tramp elsewhere to get it.

The admiration I have for George Orwell is both deep and unyielding, yet I cannot help but find his naivety here as blinding as it is uncharacteristic of a man usually so perceptive. Of course there are those who choose not to work – we have the expressions 'dossers', 'slackers' and 'benefits cheats' for a reason. I met plenty on the streets who claimed their avoidance of work came from an abhorrence of 'the system', the 'rat race', 'convention', but these were just excuses. Many of the rough sleepers I met on my journey were troubled people in need, but there were also a few who did not mind the discomfort and the squalor so long as they got to do whatever they liked all day.

Orwell called this idea of choosing-to-tramp an atavism, the re-emergence of a nomadism which he thought of as primitive and pejorative. But nomadism is neither of these. It continues to exist across the world, and nomadic cultures can be just as civilised as their settled cousins. We often have nomads to thank for the great leaps in human history: nomads discovered the importance of crop rotation long before settlers did; the nomadic Huns instigated the fall of the Roman Empire; nomads struck out and discovered the world – for were not Christopher Columbus, Captain Cook, and the pioneers and cowboys of the Wild West nomads in their own right?

There has always been, among certain folk in every country, a choice to roam. In England, those who make that choice often become tramps. And Orwell should have been more careful when he disparaged the idea, for – with all the help that he could ever need from his rich family just a telegram away – he too made his own choice to tramp.

It was a choice I decided to make myself.

5

Plenty had travelled through England and written about it. But this was not so much a journey through a country as a journey through a lifestyle. I would, I decided, walk through England, and I would walk as a tramp.

I forced myself to minimise on everything I would take. My two sets of clothes were charity-shop bought, as was the shabby knapsack they were stuffed into, alongside a pound-shop penknife, bin-bag raincoat and two tatty paperbacks: Penguin Popular Classic editions of *A Tale of Two Cities* and *Great Expectations*. I looked, by all outward appearances, a tramp, though some things gave me away. My boots were good. My tiny camping stove, a plastic spork, a few tins of beans and sausages and my warm sleeping bag were all items I perhaps should have discarded, but they were minimal luxuries I felt I could not do without on the long walk I planned.

What also gave me away, behind my patchy beard and beneath my stained cap, was my voice: a voice honed over the years as an English schoolteacher. Orwell had the same problem when he went down and out in Paris and London: when he first took to the streets in the latter city, he dared not speak for the first night, for fear others would notice the juxtaposition of his soiled and grubby clothes with his public-school, imperialist voice.

As aforementioned, the seed of this book began with Orwell, and early treatments of the idea revolved around a kind of *Down and Out in the Twenty-first Century*. But I did not want to merely follow in Orwell's footsteps about the spikes of London and kitchens of Paris. I wanted his immersive investigation, but I fancied marrying it with a nice long walk.

And so I became a tramp. I would travel like one (on foot), sleep like one (rough), and live like one (all possessions portable). No mobile phone, no laptop, no bank cards; a wallet with fifty pounds to spend on food so that I would not have to rely on begging (though I will admit I sewed an emergency hundred pounds into the lining of my shoddy jacket), a cheap digital watch, a toothbrush, fingerless gloves. Everything I carried was expendable. Only two matters remained: the route and the rules by which to travel it.

I would start, I decided, at my own Cornish front door. From there, the rest of the country lay in the same direction: north. Scottish John O'Groats was a tempting finale, but scores of thousands had done that before. *If I were a tramp*, I thought, *eager to leave Cornwall, where would I go?* The answer came immediately. *I would go to London.* London. Where the streets were paved with gold. I could be bloody Dick Whittington: bindle on a stick; mangy cat at my heels.

I scanned maps and saw a likely route. If I began on the coast, I could walk it all the way to Bristol, then forge a line east to the capital. I called a friend who lived in Portishead – on the coast, a few miles outside of Bristol – and asked if he might let me sleep on his couch for a night or two. It would be a welcome halfway pit stop.

'You make it this far on foot,' he replied, 'and you can *sell* my couch.'

Was sleeping on a couch cheating? I wondered as I put the phone down. Of course it wasn't. Tramps lived by whatever means they could. Would a tramp turn down shelter for the night if it was offered? Would a tramp ignore a free lift?

I decided on two simple rules for my journey: rules which, I supposed, all tramps lived by out of necessity – I would not pay for transport, but I would take it if it came free; I would not pay for accommodation, but nor would I dismiss an available and cost-free bed or couch – and I would live by those two rules as I tramped from Cornwall to London. This was choice.

CHAPTER TWO

CORNISH COAST

I

I had liked the alliteration of tramping from Land's End to London, but all reasons for starting at the former were arbitrary. I had been to Land's End on a score of school trips, first as a child and then as a teacher, and it held no symbolism for me. I knew all too well its faux pirate ship, its smuggling stories, its signpost which cost money to stand under. And I had a notion that I might have to pay an entrance fee just to get to that arbitrary starting point. Sennen Cove was but a few miles from Land's End, and it was far prettier. I stopped for the night at my mother's on the way.

'You've always been like this, you know,' she said over a jacket potato dinner.

'Like what?'

'Disappearing off on your little missions.'

'It's wanderlust. I like it. It's made my life interesting.'

25

'Even when you were a kid. I used to try everything to keep you from wandering off from the house and getting lost, all manner of locks and bolts, but you always escaped somehow.'

I recalled, at the age of seven, a habit I developed of getting up early in the morning, sneaking out of the house while everyone else slept, letting myself into our neighbour's house (with the spare key we kept in case of emergency), creeping past the mother's and the sister's bedrooms to wake my friend, and then walking with him around our little village while it was still dark. I used to say I liked the *smell* of the village in those hours, though I cannot for the life of me remember what it was.

'No, you were doing it long before that,' my mother corrected me. 'It was worst while we were still in Manchester.'

My family had moved from Manchester to Cornwall when I was three.

'*Exactly*! Just a little toddler, and you kept bloody *escaping*! It used to drive me crazy. It was especially worrying there because our neighbour was a wanker.'

My mother is the only person I know who uses that word in its most literal sense. Our next-door neighbour had a record of exposing himself and masturbating in public.

'That's one of the reasons we got a dog after we moved to Cornwall. I thought, at least if he wanders off the dog will follow him and look after him. And he did, as well. Good as gold, he was. Once, about ten or fifteen of us went down to Wheal Jane and you disappeared again, and all of us split up to look for you. It took us an hour, but when we did, we found you sat under a bush playing with your fingers, and Oscar sat in front guarding you. The amount of times you nearly gave me a heart attack. I used to think there was something wrong with you.' She eyed my knapsack and patchy beard. 'Sometimes, I still do.'

2

It had rained for the last three weeks: a grim and miserable wash. England could be so beautiful, but it could sometimes seem the greyest place in all the northern hemisphere. As I walked through Sennen, palm trees drooped under the early-morning clouds and, down at the beach, the tourists were already out, fully clothed and squatting behind their windbreaks, their foam surfboards anchored into the sand. At the far end of Sennen Cove, a small path led up towards the cliffs. This was the South West Coastal Path, marked with the British walking autograph: the white acorn. I followed its arrow, the first of many, beneath the granite stacks which leered over the trail, ecstatic to be on my way.

The weather seemed to meet my euphoria, for within an hour the sun came out and, to my astonishment, stayed for most of my time in Cornwall. The waters which lapped at the fringe of the coast, the coves and lagoons, turned turquoise. Purple heather and yellow gorse sealed the gentle slopes down, and buzzards circled beneath my feet, bleating their signature three staccato, piercing shrieks. This aesthetic advantage was one of my reasons for beginning the tramp here, but the north coast of Cornwall also gave me time to find my feet. The whole distance was scored by a National Trust footpath; wild sleeping was easy and safe.

A group of two women and two children sunbathed on rocks jutting out from the path. They saw me as I rounded a headland. Though I was far away, I could tell from their swivelled heads that their eyes were following me as I approached. When it was clear I was going to reach them, they stood up to leave, gathering their belongings in their arms. I knew what I looked like: a tramp, it was purposeful. I was still clean and I did not yet smell, but the power of one's clothes is robust. Orwell noted that, when he first wore tramp's clothes, he felt like they thrust him into a different world, one where women shudder, men scoff, and other street-fellows start to call you 'mate'. He compared the sudden plunge into shame to a first night in prison.

Today, in the cities, tramp's clothes are like magic: they make you invisible. To all, that is, except those others dressed like you. *They* notice you – they nod, they smile, they do not ask for spare change or offer a copy of *The Big Issue*, and you begin to realise that, in fact, they had always noticed you. But, until now, they had been invisible to you. In the countryside, it is different. Tramps are not found there any more. Anyone dressed like a tramp in the countryside must be, categorically, a 'weirdo'.

As we crossed paths, the two children and the first woman kept their eyes fastened to the ground. The second stared coolly at me.

'Is this the right path to Cape Cornwall?' I asked. There was another below.

'Yes, it is,' she replied, her sudden relief apparent.

I was soon to learn that, while my clothes had power, so too did my accent.

Sennen Cove stayed present and visible behind me from every headland I circumnavigated. After two hours, I reached Cape Cornwall and, as I turned my first corner, Sennen disappeared for the last time. The environment seemed to change, too – the wind rose; turquoise lagoons turned to blue surf; engine houses rode the cliffs' peaks while ventilation shafts poked out on to the footpath, eerie and black as death. I was no longer walking north, but east.

Beyond the Pendeen Watch lighthouse, I crossed the waterfall at Portheras beach and then ascended a killing climb. It was late morning, the sun was ferocious, and I was exhausted already. I needed a break. An old German gentleman who spoke with a Scottish accent hovered at the turn-off to Morvah.

'Do you know how far it is to Morvah?' I asked.

'Only five minutes. Where have you walked from?'

'Today, Sennen.'

'Yes, me too. Have you seen any beaches near here?'

'There's one back over that headland,' I said, pointing behind me at Portheras.

'*No!*' he snapped. 'I do *not* mean Pendeen!'

'Sorry.'

'They say Morvah beach is the best beach on the coast. But they will not tell me where it is. It is a well-kept secret. No matter. I *will* find it.' He widened his eyes and grinned a manic leer with the last sentence.

I left him there to resume his circles, and walked into Morvah in search of water. Already, my two litres were gone. The owner of a local tea shop let me fill my bottle from her tap. I gulped down half the bottle, refilled it again, and then stepped outside to lie back on a bank of grass to rest. My feet ached and I was still miles from Gwithian, where I had hoped to spend the night. I considered catching a bus there, I could afford it, but that would be 'against the rules', as arbitrary as they were. Didn't tramps ever catch buses?

What I could do, I contemplated, was hitch-hike. It would likely be a fruitless enterprise – a recent study had been published which revealed that less people than ever before were willing to stop for hitch-hikers – but I could at least try. Hobbling over to the main road, a thin and twisting snake of concrete, I sat at the edge and raised my thumb each time a car passed.

Half an hour later, a rented Mini Cooper stopped, and the passenger door swung open. I climbed in and turned to smile at the driver. It was the German. He grimaced when he recognised me.

'They lied to me,' he said. 'It was the beach you referred to. This has made me very angry.'

He was driving to St Ives, and agreed to drop me off at the far end of town. His temper flashed and snarled each time we were forced to stop upon the narrow road while another car passed, and the open-top tourist bus which forced him to reverse a few metres really sent him over the edge. He shouted at it in German as it squeezed past us. I was glad to bid him farewell in St Ives.

My feet now rested and recovered, I walked the long route around the Hayle estuary – following the road, bored – to Mexico Towans and then Gwithian. I knew this beach well. It had miles of labyrinthine sand dunes which I could disappear into for the night, and I walked into them to cook my dinner: beans and sausages in a mess tin. It tasted sensational.

There was a campsite nearby and I stole on to it to fill my water bottle and wash out my mess tin. Back in the dunes I made camp: my sleeping bag tucked into the corner of a sandy caldera. I swapped my cap for my woolly hat with earflaps and sat on the lip of my little volcano to watch a cloudless sunset over the Atlantic. Rabbits scattered into their dune-warrens as I stepped up and then reappeared a few moments later as I sat still. Tonight, I thought, I will sleep with the bunnies.

3

I stayed atop the dune long after the sun had set, waiting for the few people who dotted the sandy peaks to leave, for the camper vans in the nearby car park to either drive away or close their curtains. I wished I had my camper van. The temperature dropped sharply and I began to shiver, but the harmless-looking couple sat two dunes in front of me would likely pass back this way, and I wanted no one to see me in my sleeping bag.

Of all the circumstances and situations I had anticipated for my journey, this – my first night sleeping rough – was the one I had feared the most. Not that this was by any homeless standards 'rough': the beach at my feet, the dune-walls for shelter, my sleeping bag for warmth and coat for pillow, this was bloody luxury. Regardless, I was afraid. The night would be a defining one. If it passed without hindrance, I knew I could do this. But if it did not – if it was too cold to bear, if a rat crawled over my face or an adder wormed its way into my sleeping bag – I would likely catch the next bus home.

What worried me most was discovery. An irate landowner perhaps (someone had to own these dunes, *all* land in England was owned) or, worse, piss-heads: here for an after-dark session of tinned lager, who would happen upon me asleep, surround me, kick me, and laugh.

As the couple finally left, walking slowly towards the campsite, I climbed into my sleeping bag, fully clothed, torch and penknife to hand's reach in my pocket. Sealing the fabric so tightly around me that only my eyes, nose and mouth remained uncovered, I lay flat on my back and closed my eyes. The fatigue of a day's walking pressed in, but sleep was difficult. I was cold and uncomfortable, and as the hours passed I grew colder and more uncomfortable, twisting inside my sleeping bag to cover my chilled face or relieve a limb numbed from the hard ground – contrary to my beliefs, sand was not nature's divan – then twisting back again because the disproportionate shifts of the sleeping bag had somehow secured my arm in an unnatural position behind my back.

The temperature continued to plummet in inverse relation to my lassitude, so that when the night was coolest I was at my most awake. It was August, I was in Cornwall in a sleeping bag, and I was cold. If I could not sleep through this, how did the homeless ever manage at the height of winter in the northern cities with only a few sheets of cardboard for insulation? The answer was, of course, that many did not – hypothermia is one of the most common killers amongst the homeless, alongside drug overdoses and suicide. It is little surprise that the life expectancy of the average rough sleeper is forty-two years.

I slept little, perhaps two hours at the most, stolen in brief snatches when my mind finally, blissfully wandered, interrupted minutes later by twitches and starts which brought me back to full consciousness. Rough sleeping would, I understood, take some getting used to. In fact, I achieved very few full good nights' sleep while I was tramping, not in the usual sense of the phrase. Few do. It is perhaps why many homeless drink so much and take so many drugs: to get through the night, the tramp's natural enemy. One can get used to almost anything, but I never learned to get past that, and my sleeping patterns remained fragmented, patchy and sporadic for as long as I stayed outside.

At least early starts on the coast were easy: the dawn chorus of seagulls which erupted soon after five o'clock became my seaside alarm. Packing my sleeping bag into its small sack, I climbed down the dunes and walked across Gwithian beach, over the river, and then back up on to the coast path. After a cereal bar for breakfast, I cleaned my teeth looking out over Godrevy Point lighthouse, Virginia Woolf's favourite, the rising sun glinting off St Ives windows across the bay. The throbbing headache of sleep deprivation melted away, replaced by a surge of exhilaration. Why, I thought, doesn't everyone tramp?

4

I drew closer to the Cornwall I knew, not Penwith but Carrick. Vast panoramas appeared in the way that they can in Cornwall, so that all at once I could see the houses of Camborne spilling into their valley, the proud Carn Brea Monument, St Agnes Beacon and the far headland of Perranporth. As I walked, I deliberated over whether I should conceive a 'backstory'. Every homeless person has their origin myth, the trauma or mistake or addiction which first put them on the streets.

I'm Richard Dawson. My wife left me and took the house. I turned to drink and lost my job. With no money and no family, I ended up on the streets. At least I could drink there.

But I was reluctant to lie. My last journey through England had in its own way involved subterfuge, and this had left a taste of guilt. Why not just be honest this time? *I'm Charlie Carroll. I'm happily married, and I'm walking to London. I'm writing a book about tramping.*

The problem with telling someone you were writing a book was that it had a similar effect to pointing a camera in their face. They froze, or acted weird, or bombarded you with irrelevant stories or, worse, jokes, which they insisted would be 'great material for your book'. In short, they stopped acting themselves: anathema to the non-fiction writer.

In Portreath, I stopped at a bench to boil some noodles for lunch. An old gentleman walking his friendly collie sat next to me.

'Glorious morning,' he said. 'Not the best I've seen, but always a treat. Especially these last few years, when summer's been such a washout. You a rambler?' He pointed at my knapsack.

'Kind of,' I replied.

'I used to walk a lot when I was younger. And cycle. Once cycled from Plymouth to Birmingham. No particular reason. Now I like boats. I had one in Falmouth for a while. Bloody beauty, she was. But couldn't afford to keep her when I retired. What do you do?'

'I'm a writer. It's what I'm doing now. Writing a book about walking.'

'All the best, then!' he said, suddenly rising to his feet, whistling to his dog, and striding away.

My favourite stretch of the Cornish northern coast begins at Portreath and finishes at Perranporth. I was pleased I had left so early that morning, for my digital watch revealed that there were still enough hours left in the day to complete the 10 miles between the two beaches. This single portion is like a Cornwall in miniature, filled with the sheer cliffs, golden beaches, engine houses, sky, wind and waves which one imagines when Cornwall is cited. It is the land of *wheals* (Cornish for 'workplace') and *porths* (Cornish for 'port' or 'beach'). Semantic anglicisation dissipates around these parts, and ancient Kernewek rejoices in its stead.

By Tre, Ros, Pol, Lan, Car and Pen,
Shall ye know most Cornishmen.

These are the Cornish prefixes, rooted in the indigenous, but now obsolete, Gaelic language of Kernewek. Like the Welsh, Scottish and Irish languages alongside it, Kernewek was a distinct – though not dissimilar – Celtic derivative. As England's kingdom expanded and sought to empower itself through the generalisation of language, no small redemptions were left for Kernewek (or Cornish, if we are to continue the philological subjugation) as they were for the Welsh language, which was allowed its own translations of the Bible and the Prayer Book. Likewise, no renaissance took place in Cornwall as it did in other areas such as the *gaeltacht* of western Ireland. The old kingdom of Kernow, it seems, was just too insignificant for such movements.

The language died with an alarming rapidity. Most authorities celebrate the last official speaker of Kernewek as one Dolly Pentreath from Mousehole (pronounced 'Mauz-all'), who took the language with her when she died at the age of 102 in 1777, though in Zennor one can find a church-wall plaque in memory of John Davey of Boswednack, died 1891, who many claim to have been the last true Cornish speaker.

Though Cornish nationalism has heightened somewhat over the last few decades, any renaissance of Kernewek still seems a long way off, destined to end perhaps right at its taking-off point, within the subservient *a'gas dynergh* ('Welcome to...') of a town sign. Kernewek has indubitably fallen to (and, perhaps, will never rise from) its own proverb: *Mez den heb davas a-gollas y-dir*. The man who loses his tongue loses his land.

The wind mounted as I climbed the shaley paths up from each porth so that my lips cracked and my cheeks stung while I scree-walked down again to the next. There are three or four interlocking paths on this section of the coast, but I, according with my childhood preferences, chose the ones which ran along the edge, the ones which spilled over on to fifty-foot vertical drops, devoid of fences or protective barriers, there being no point for such objects, as they would only fall down the cliffs themselves after a few years. I remembered stories my parents used to tell when we came up here for family walks, parables perhaps, cautionary warnings of dogs who had blithely chased thrown stones out over the edge to plummet down to the rocks below. There were further stories of the same bent, ones which kept us away from the conical metal tips which presided over the obsolete mineshafts. 'Only three years ago, a girl fell down that one there. They say she landed in a pile of skeletons and died of fright.'

I came to Wheal Coates, the magnificently preserved engine house which stands as the archetype for all the mine works dotted up and down the coast. Wheal Coates is not especially old, but it looks as ancient as the cliffs themselves. Only a few generations ago, people worked here, but we are so distanced from them that they might as well have been the same folk who erected the Men-an-Tol.

I suppose in many ways they were. The mining tradition in Cornwall can be dated back as far as 1800 BC, when Bronze Age tinners worked above ground, locating exposed veins of ore and streaming the tin from the rock face. By 400 BC, the quality of Cornish tin was famed across Europe: it was shipped across the English Channel to Gaul, where it was then carried on horseback to the Carthaginians and the Greeks who used it to make bronze, the war metal. By the fifteenth century, work moved below the surface, and the tinners evolved into miners. Cornish mining became a booming industry, its success owed to the skill of the workers and the abundance of the tin. At one point, almost a third of the world's tin came from Cornwall.

It was not until the nineteenth century that the last great age of mining came, and then died. Copper was discovered. Work soared to meet international demands: almost fifty thousand Cornish worked full-time down the mines; and Cornwall became the largest area for copper production in the world, producing two-thirds of the global supply. But then tragedy hit in the 1860s. Heady amounts of copper were discovered in Africa, tin in South-East Asia, and, within just a few decades, the annual production of copper in Cornwall fell from 160,000 tonnes to less than five hundred. One by one, the mines were systematically shut down. The miners responded with exodus, fleeing to distant corners of the globe to continue doing the only thing they knew, the only thing their families had known for 3,000 years. Today, the few people you will see around the old, disused engine houses and chimneys are tourists, or, like me, locals who are little more than tourists of history. For it is all history now. Today, not one mine in Cornwall remains open.

Seagulls circled and screeched angrily overhead as I continued on towards Trevaunance Cove and then Perranporth. It was as far as I planned to go for the day, and I was glad, for I could walk no further. My feet had raged for miles, but far worse was the pain from my chafing thighs which was fast growing indescribable. I allowed myself the luxury purchase of a small tub of moisturiser.

It was not yet evening in Perranporth, and I had a few hours to kill before wandering off into the dunes to sleep, so I walked through the village to knock on the door of my old friend Ben, who kindly cooked me a dinner so large I wolfed it down and then immediately regretted my haste. Ben owned a restaurant in St Agnes. I had passed it two hours before and noticed it was busy.

'Been a good season,' Ben confirmed. 'I've reduced evening turnover and maximised on lunches instead. Profits are up.'

Such was the sociolect of many modern Cornish: talk of seasons and profits, covers and turnover was the new Kernewek, for tourism was the new mining.

Another favourite conversation piece was second homes. Many of Cornwall's houses, especially those along the coast, have been bought up for astonishing prices by people who live in them for less than six weeks a year. This has pushed property prices in the county up to one of the highest averages in England, so that today fewer Cornish people own their own homes than ever before. As house prices have risen with the second-home culture, so too has rent, though average salaries have not. As a result, there has been a marked increase in Cornwall's homeless population over the past decade.

'Have you heard of *mundic*?' Ben asked.

'No,' I admitted.

'One of my favourite anecdotes is about second homes and mundic. You know that row of houses looking over Trevaunance Cove from the cliffs at the west end?'

I nodded. I had walked past them a few hours earlier.

'Over the last ten years they've all been bought up as second homes. Some of them are prone to mundic. Mundic is a phenomenon you only get in a few pockets of the West Country. It's a property that can be found in building materials, and it acts like a kind of rust for stone. Mundic's untreatable, too, and in most cases it'll end up reducing a house to rubble. All houses diagnosed with mundic have been given terminal sentences, and they're not eligible for a mortgage. The last of those houses on the cliffs above Trevaunance Cove, it was riddled with mundic, and it just got sold for £1.2 million.'

I whistled in astonishment.

'No mortgage there,' Ben reminded me. 'It was sold for *cash*.'

5

I bedded down within Perranporth's dunes at ten o'clock at night, and then rose with the sun the following morning. I had spent the night, again, chasing sleep, but only managing perhaps an hour or two. The lack of true rest left me irritable and profoundly bad-tempered. I had *walked* here from Sennen! I was *exhausted*! Why the *fuck* was I not sleeping better? I could even doze right now, if it weren't for those *bastard* seagulls and their *constant fucking bleating*. I angrily unwrapped a cereal bar, daring one of the hovering birds to come closer so that I could punch it in the beak.

Within minutes of walking, I was fine again. It was a template I was to grow used to as I tramped: little sleep, rude awakening, 'temper, temper', all calm. As I rounded Holywell Bay, a short bank of rain hit. The mossy grass skirting the footpath which had before seemed so soft and warm now appeared spiky and stiff; the six-foot surf rumbled through the caves and sounded a crashing tattoo against the cliff walls below me. I donned my cheap, plastic poncho – the kind sold at tourist attractions and festivals from mobile stalls – and wrapped my knapsack in the bin bag I kept it in at night to keep it dry from dew, and I strode on to Newquay. Though the weather kept the tourists and the walkers indoors, it replaced them with wildlife. A seal bobbed in the calm recesses of an inaccessible cove, head above the water, eyes blinking, and three rare Cornish choughs – identifiable by their red bills and red legs, but mostly by the tags stapled above their little feet – barked furiously at me as I passed.

At the far end of Crantock beach, the River Gannel barred my route to Newquay. It had taken me hours to walk around the Hayle estuary two days before when a neat bridge would have shortened the journey to fifteen minutes, and I was reluctant to repeat the experience here. A man in a hoodie, shorts and a moustache ran people across in his small outrigger dinghy for £1.20, his large dog at the bow like a formidable bust, paws on the rim. I broke my rules, paid the man, and climbed in. The dog eyed me with distrust, settled down for a nap as we set off across the water, and then bolted back to the bow a minute later as we reached the far side to make sure I got off.

All along the coast, each village or small town had been a welcome break from the wilderness of the cliffs: places to rest, buy a cup of tea or top up my small stock of food in packets and tins – more beans, more noodles, more bread. But Newquay, that foul Balearic wannabe, was excruciating. I hoped to pass it as quickly as possible, but I had forgotten how big it was. It just kept going, beach after beach – Fistral, Towan, Great Western, Tolcarne, Lusty Glaze – and then, further on, others which were places in their own right – Porth, Watergate Bay, Mawgan Porth – though they seemed to have been subsumed into the Newquay leviathan. I had unpleasant memories as I walked through: this was the catchment area of a school at which I had been bullied.

Newquay was always charmless and dreary, but at some point in the eighties the retirees and the bathers abandoned it either for or because of a new breed of tourist. Which came first, the holiday camp or the family of drunken parents and screaming children? The five-storey nightclub or the stag party? The chain pub or the street brawl? Such questions are immaterial, the result is the same. Newquay, historically depressing, has somehow become *more* depressing: a claustrophobic vista of bellies, breasts, *Daily Star* readers, testosterone, and sunburned flesh. It is the saliva fleck on Cornwall's cheek, the drunken punch-up of the wedding.

It was already mid afternoon by the time I reached Mawgan Porth; the clouds had cleared, the sun blazed, and so did my feet. I had covered the least amount of miles that day, and I could not go much further. I resolved to eat and rest a while before making camp a few miles along the cliffs.

Mawgan Porth was a cavernous beach, the steep valley sides ensnaring the heat so that it felt like flames licked across the sand. The bars and cafes, the single pub, were filled with tourists, and queues streamed from the fish and chip shops and ice-cream stands. All the men seemed to be skinheads, all the women had too much make-up around their eyes, and all the children were sunburned.

It was quietest at the northern end of the beach, where subsidence had left a shallow cave exposed in the overgrown cliff face, like a bite from an apple. I weaved through the windbreaks and deckchairs, the surf schools and semi-naked septuagenarians, to the privacy of the far corner, where I stretched out on my bed of soft, hot sand. With no wind, I cooked quickly and then, feeling drowsy, lay back with my book, asleep in minutes.

I believe I slept for over an hour, though it was one of those slumbers which pass in an instant and feel like a blink. Letting my book fall to my side, I had closed my eyes to nothing but blue sky. When I opened them again, three men stood over me.

They each looked no older than twenty, had dirty hair and hands, and that strikingly indicative sartorial combination of jeans and no top. Their expensive trainers were coated in sand. They were drinking and they were drunk: cans of lager poked out of pockets and dribbled from hands. One dangled my camping stove, which I had forgotten to pack away, over my face.

'How much for this?' he asked. I stared at the silhouette of his head, trying hard to discern his features against the bright sky. An orange and white passenger jet flew from his ear.

'It's not for sale,' I said, pulling myself to my feet. I was taller than each of them, but, though they were lean, there was a look of self-confidence in their eyes which I did not like.

'Come on, mate, we'll give you a good price,' another said. I knew their accents. They were not tourists, but local boys.

'How much?' I asked out of curiosity, beginning to gather my things.

'I'll give you a fiver for it.'

I laughed. 'No, thanks,' I said, reaching out to take the stove.

The man holding it stepped back as I reached forward, and his friend took a step closer to me.

'Come on, mate,' he said. 'You look like you could do with the money.'

He was too close to me now: he meant to be threatening. The one who held the stove stared at me. The third did not make eye contact, looked uncomfortable, but his feet were firmly rooted, and an appeal to him would be useless. The nearest family were too far away to hear anything, but close enough to run to. Even if I did, and even if these men gave chase, would the tourists here even care? Maybe they would simply stand back and watch. A story to tell back home. The Tramp versus the Chavs.

'I don't need the money,' I said, shouldering my knapsack. 'But I need that stove.'

'Bet you do,' he said, and then: 'fucking tramp.'

A number of very odd things happened at that moment. First, a cascade of emotions surged through me: base fear was primary, but behind it I noticed an inappropriate flash of elation. He had called me a tramp! I looked the part! Following that came a sense of absurdity, and then finally fear again.

The second odd thing: the man holding my stove lit it, and pointed the flame at me. The surrealism of it all overwhelmed me: *threatened with my own camping stove.*

I had enough will left for one last attempt. 'Can I have that back?' I asked.

There was no reply. Instead, the man played with the single dial, turning the gas output up to maximum. The flame roared.

That was enough. I walked around the man who still stood so close to me I could smell the alcohol on his breath, careful not to barge him with my shoulder or knock him with my bag, and headed towards the nearest family as quickly as I could without seeming panicked. There were times in travel when this was the only answer, and I felt no shame in the action.

'Oi!' a voice shouted from behind me. I continued walking. 'Oi!' it called again, and I heard feet thumping on the sand. I stopped. Turned.

'You forgot this, you twat.' He threw the camping stove, still alight, towards me. It landed harmlessly in the sand a few feet to my right: his poor aim had, I think, been deliberate. That made me feel better. These boys were keen to intimidate, but not drunk enough for violence. I bent down, turned the gas off, picked up the stove and then continued to walk back towards the masses of people. The coast path lay in the opposite direction, but I wanted to lose the three of them before climbing up on to it, alone.

6

Further days and nights passed as I trudged the coast path. Already, the slow pace of long-distance walking was beginning to frustrate me: if I had driven for as many hours as I had walked, I could be in Eastern Europe by now. The going was hot and arduous, the flat straights were all but disappearing as I walked further north, and the unremitting plunges and rises had slowed me to as little as one or two miles an hour. Between Port Isaac and Boscastle, I faced my toughest portion yet: 15 miles of steep inclines and declines, one after the other. The path had narrowed to a thin dirt track, sprinkled in loose pebbles, which caused jolts of panic whenever it lay but a few centimetres from the edge of a sheer, stark cliff face. After the fifth rise, I began to grunt like a tennis player with each step up; after the tenth, I believe I stopped thinking altogether. Life became automation.

Limping into Boscastle, I spent a long while sat on a bench with my shoes removed. I had hoped to make it to Bude and the Cornwall-Devon border by late evening, but I had no energy to stay anywhere other than here for the night.

Boscastle was all but destroyed by a flood in 2004, and later rebuilt as identical as possible to its former self – with the addition of extra flood-prevention measures, of course. I had been in Abu Dhabi airport that day, and I remember almost dropping my glass of lager when on the bar's TV screen, below the images of what appeared to be yet another tragic catastrophe in the developing world, the name 'Boscastle' flashed up. It was not the Mekong or the Yangtze or the Amazon which was tearing down those buildings like paper, it was the River Valency, just a few miles from my home a quarter of the world away.

Unlike its Devonshire flood-cousin Lynmouth, Boscastle is not filled with plaques denoting heights and depths. There are framed photographs on shop and pub walls of the river surging over cars and into windows, but these seem accepting, boastful even, rather than sad or recriminating. Perhaps this is because, unlike Lynmouth, nobody died in the Boscastle flood. Alongside the mouth of the Valency at the harbour, four large stalks of driftwood lie as rudimentary benches. Across them is inscribed a poem of admiration rather than fear:

Ledrow a dherow ow nedha
War-nans golans glas Velinji
Dhe borth saw Atlantek garow
Giver ow kwoffi a fros rybon.

Twisting oak slopes
Down verdant Valency
To harbour haven Atlantic swell
Rising river rushes by.

The sun had scorched the back of my neck all day, but at Tintagel clouds had wafted in from the sea and the temperature had dropped. The night up on the cliffs would, I knew, be a cold one, and so, after a dinner of soup, I walked into the village for a pot of hot tea to warm my blood. It would cost money I did not want to spend, but the sacrifice would be worth it.

The Harbour Light Tea Garden had been destroyed by the flood but, in its rebuilt condition, with its bowed roof and lopsided slant, it could easily have been mistaken for its former sixteenth-century self. There I fell to talking with Michael, who was staying at the youth hostel next door and had come in for dinner. Michael was one of those men in their sixties who believe everything they say to be of the utmost fascination. These men do not digress or go off on a tangent: moreover, they bludgeon a subject remorselessly until every last vestige of it, and of the listener's interest, is spent. These men will rarely look you in the eye while they speak – for, if they did, they would surely discern their companion's boredom or desperation to leave, and would thereby shut up.

Michael was also on a grand trip, cycling the entire British coast on a recumbent trike: a three-wheeled, fluorescent-yellow hive of flags and horns, upon which he sat back and pedalled, steering from handlebars by his hips. His monologue was one of numbers, gradients, obscure place-names and incomprehensible jargon.

'Passing through Blaencelyn, on the road between Nanternis and Penbryn, I was on a four-in-one, then a two-pointer incline, easy enough at a ten-mile-an-hour constant and with my derailleurs and dual-pivots, though I should have got V-types, but that's by the by, when my lumbar support dropped, sending me into a spin of about eighty, maybe even ninety, no, not ninety, eighty-five max, smack bang into a road sign, not your average flat-top sheeting, but reinforced concrete, about six point four. Luckily, I was able to buy a new top-tube from a parts shop in Blaencelyn, second-right off the main street, between the Gregg's and the PDSA charity shop, which only cost me eighty-seven pounds, when I know that my guy at home, who hasn't ripped me off once, couldn't get it for less than ninety-three, and that's only if he does it off the books, which he does sometimes, but not as often as I might like. Now my trike's fine again, and I've added some nice six by sevens.'

'Can you do a wheelie on it?' I asked.

It would have been pleasant to spend the evening in the Harbour Light with my tea and a book, but Michael was dull and his monologue devoid of lengthy pauses, so I escaped when I saw the chance – at the conclusion of a twenty-minute description of his tent.

I wanted to call my wife to let her know how far I had walked, but both public payphones in Boscastle only accepted credit cards, and I did not have one. Instead, I entered a restaurant and asked the teenage waiter if he knew of any cash payphones in the area. The manager, a quiet and superior fellow, appeared, and the waiter asked him if I might use the restaurant's phone. The manager stared at me, contempt discernible on his pudgy face, and then turned and walked into the kitchen.

'I'll just make sure it's all right,' the waiter said, following him. He reappeared moments later. 'Sorry, mate,' he said. 'I've been told to ask you to leave.'

7

I left Boscastle through its harbour on my way back to the cliffs. A family from Yorkshire stood on the quay while their two sons dangled crab-lines into the water. They were talking to a Cornish father and son who were clearing their boat after a day's fishing. Together, they had found their common ground.

'Better living here than London.'

'You couldn't pay me enough to live in London.'

'Lot of young lads round our way head to London to make their fortune. They're soon back.'

'Streets are paved with shite.'

The sunset from the cliff-top was magnificent, but the night which followed was far colder than it had been yet, and I donned both my T-shirts and pairs of trousers along with my sweatshirt and jacket, so that I could barely move inside my sleeping bag. Sleep was as fragmented and unsatisfying as ever, and the few dreams I had featured wide and empty landscapes which dipped and rose like waves to the horizon.

The next morning remained dark and cloudy. Birds beat their wings against the brutal whips and shoves of the wind. The sun rose, but it was difficult to notice. Visibility was awful, and I was lucky if I could see the next headland. The beaches below had turned to grey shale. I crossed Widemouth Bay, deserted and moon-like, the low tide far away, its messy waves closing out under the onshore wind.

Such conditions cemented a notion that had been building for a while: that perhaps it was time to leave the coast. I had had enough of the ankle-twisting pathway, the back-breaking ascents and the thigh-bursting descents, and the omnipresent clamouring of seagulls had begun to irritate me. I would miss the sea, of course, but if I followed this path for long enough even that would morph into the gravy of the Bristol Channel.

Anyway, Cornwall *was* its coast, and I was about to leave it, so why not the coast, too? Until as late as Victorian times, some Londoners referred to Cornwall as West Barbary. It no longer applies to the Cornish, but it can perhaps still be said of the land. The barbarism of Cornwall is ravishing, but not when you lack a bed. Devon was different: it was rolling hills, country roads, civilisation. As I summited the final headland, the sun came out, and Bude, all low roofs, opened up before me in the valley, behind it the giant satellites of the Earth Station and, offshore, Lundy Island. I walked down into Bude, and left the coast path.

CHAPTER THREE

DEVONSHIRE ROADS

I

'Hey! Buddy! All right? All *right*!' He was smiling, and the smile grew broader when he realised I was going to stop. Few did. 'Alex,' he said, wrenching my hand from my side and shaking it enthusiastically as I told him my name. Often, I did not stop for charity street-hawkers, not since I heard that they earned a commission for each person they signed up to donate. That struck me as rather uncharitable. But now I had all the time in the world to stop and chat, and Alex – in his black T-shirt with 'POVERTY' emblazoned across his chest – seemed friendly. 'What you up to today?'

'Walking,' I replied.

'Just walking?'

'Pretty much.'

'Where have you walked from?'

'Sennen.'

'Wow, man, that's like miles. That's really cool. So, what, are you just staying in hostels, B and Bs, that kind of thing?'

'No,' I said, hesitating over semantics. 'I, err, I sleep rough mostly.'

Alex's smile began to fade. 'That must get pretty cold,' he faltered.

'I've got a sleeping bag,' I said, turning around and gesturing to the pouch tied to my knapsack. 'I'm luckier than most.'

'Hey, man, well good luck to you, you know?' he said. Already, his eyes were scanning the passing tourists for likely candidates.

'Yeah. Thanks.' I walked away.

Alex did not say goodbye.

I was not homeless, but by now, after over a week walking and sleeping rough, my clothes dirty and pungent, my face browned but unshaven, I looked homeless. Though I had not explicitly stated it, Alex had inferred as such, and I knew it and had done nothing to dissuade him. And, with his clipboard, his charity wristbands, his winning, altruistic smile, he had been of as little help as the Boscastle restaurant manager. There was, I decided, very little that was charitable about Alex.

2

A terrific ache had set in along my thigh muscles and, though I had not walked far from Boscastle to Bude, my feet already felt like they were going to burst from my shoes. I had pushed myself too hard the day before and knew it would not be wise to do the same today. John Hillaby, who made a literary career out of walking, used to say that he treated his feet like premature twins. I had not afforded mine the same precious quality, though I should have, for there is little save perhaps the heart which is more important to the walker. Accordingly, I decided to break for the day, rest up, and continue tomorrow.

It was only midday and so I walked down to the beach to make lunch. The sun was peaking and, now that I did not have to worry about movement and drinking-water, I could enjoy it. Down at the shore, I washed my mess tin and then, feeling brave, stripped to my underwear and plunged into the waves, splashing and rinsing from my feet to my eyebrows. The exercise was psychosomatic: I was not cleaning – if anything, the stench of the sea and the crust of salt would make me smell worse – but the touch of water on my skin was blissful. Pulling the small towel from the bottom of my knapsack, I wrapped it around my waist and wandered off to find a quiet spot on the beach, where I changed my underwear, laid the saturated pair out beside me to dry, and then lay back to slip into a sleep deeper than any yet.

When I awoke two hours later, it was with a shiver. Clouds shifted across the sky in erratic manoeuvres, casting long shadows across the beach. A film of sand clung to my torso and I hurriedly scraped it off so I could dress – it was cold enough to merit my sweatshirt and hat. My feet, which before had been little fires at the ends of my legs, were now as pale as frozen chicken. The approach of autumn was in the air. A few spots of rain hit the backs of my hands.

I felt invigorated and ready to move again, but I knew I should rest properly and see the day out in Bude. My only problem was that I had no idea what to do with myself. It is very difficult to rest when you have no house or shelter to rest in. Resting involves privacy, warmth, food and drink, perhaps some easy distraction: a book, a film, a newspaper. The tramp has none of these things. His life is always public, his warmth fleeting and his food and drink likewise. Distractions are rife but they are rarely leisurely. There is no television. Books cost money better spent on food, and, though he can visit the local library, the tramp cannot join it, for membership requires an address. Newspapers are good, but more effective when stuffed down trousers to keep the legs warm.

Life on the streets is not just difficult; it can also be deeply boring. I had supposed many homeless drank and abused drugs so much to be able to sleep; but maybe it was also just something to do. We all need hobbies. I considered buying eight cans of lager from the supermarket and getting horribly drunk alone down at the beach, but the prospect of walking with a hangover expelled the idea from my mind.

Instead, I spent the afternoon wandering the small town, listless and sullen, the hours dragging by as slow as fatigue. I poked my head into shops, but the employees gave me suspicious looks, and anyway what was the point if I couldn't afford anything? There was a small grassy square, but it had grown too cold to sit still. I used a public toilet to defecate and ended up sat there for the next half-hour, trousers around ankles, reading the graffiti which spiralled about the walls. I looked for homeless people who might talk to me, tell me their story or recommend a good place to spend the night, but found none. I did not doubt Bude had its homeless population – it was small, but not small enough – but of where they had hidden for the day I was ignorant. A young man in his early twenties busked outside a bakery, a few coins in his guitar-case, a backpack propped against the wall. I gave him a smile and stood next to him – we could talk about busking, if anything had changed in the last ten years – but he seemed nervous at my arrival, kept looking down at his earnings at his feet, and I was sure he was extending the song to twice the length it was supposed to be. When the eighth chorus came around, I felt stupid and awkward, and left him alone. Even Alex the charity-hawker had gone home. *Home*.

I decided to walk back along the coast path towards Widemouth Bay. Halfway between it and Bude, I had noticed a depression above the cliff face where I could sit or lie just out of view of the walkers on the path. The grass was spongy and comfortable, the view sensational and the privacy welcoming. I worried about its proximity to the cliff edge – I had always made sure to sleep well back from any drops for fear I might roll over in my sleep – but it did not matter. Owing to my afternoon nap, I did not sleep at all that night.

3

I left Bude gnawing on a cheap stick of supermarket bread, taken from the shelves and placed in a rack by the doorway, its yellow sticker the symbol of its retirement. I had to walk uphill to get out, but the gradient was nothing compared to the hellish day between Port Isaac and Boscastle. Besides, here there were pavements – the whole 2 miles to Stratton, no less! – and my feet skipped lightly over the tarmac. I joined a cycle path which would take me to Hatherleigh on the edge of Dartmoor, stopping halfway along at Holsworthy to eat lunch on a railway bridge, built in 1898, its tracks macadamed over, which rose high above a thin river. It had been the most pleasant day of walking so far.

The walker often has the smug fallacy that he is the only one going in his direction. Everybody one meets, of course, is going the other way. I had formulated and revised my classifications of other walkers since leaving Sennen, and most fell into typical camps. Artists and photographers were common, though only on the clear days, and usually in the most remote spots. I rarely, however, saw one painting or taking a photograph – more often they were walking, easel or tripod under arm, pacing back and forth until they found their subjective perfection, like a dog's ever-shrinking circles as it settles down to sleep.

Dogs were, of course, common too, walked most often early in the morning, sometimes out and on the paths before I was, usually at a beach and, if not, close to one. Protective dogs would approach me from afar, circle behind and then track me back to their owners; the more friendly dogs stuck their wet noses into my palm and then loped alongside me until their owners had to call them back, as if in fear their dog might accompany me to the horizon.

The most numerous of all, and the most indefatigable, were the ramblers: often older, ruddy and decked out in expensive all-weather-all-terrain equipment. They had swarmed the Cornish coast path like paparazzi around a celebrity, filling it with the fluorescent colours of their raincoats and the clinking melodies of their walking sticks, offset to the ambient beat of thick boots clunking on the soft ground. But, as I pushed deeper into Devon, they dissolved. In fact, the further I walked the fewer people I saw, until I began to wonder if I *was* the only one walking along this path. There had been moments of extraordinary solitude in Cornwall, when I could see no other person about, and I could almost always see far. But a town or a village was never more than a few hours away, and they heaved with summer holidaymakers. Perhaps they had all come from south Devon, for between Holsworthy and Hatherleigh I crossed paths with only a handful of people – most of them small groups of teenage boys who leaned their BMXs against a hedge and sat cross-legged on the grass sharing a pack of cigarettes between them, who paid me no heed – and, with Cornwall further and further behind me, I began to feel lonely.

4

Margaret didn't believe me. 'Promise me you'll get a good meal tonight,' she said, holding out a five-pound note.

'You're kind, but I don't need it,' I replied. 'Honestly.'

'A young man like you shouldn't be walking around with no food in his belly. Take it.'

I opened my knapsack to show her my stove and tins of beans. She brushed it aside.

'What kind of a meal is that? Take this and get yourself something proper.'

Margaret's insistence was so sweet I felt like crying. I had told her everything, but she had watched me as I spoke with a mixture of condescension and pity, and I knew none of it was taken seriously.

'It's hard for young people today,' she said, still holding out the note. 'No work, no hope for it. Do your parents know where you are?'

I smiled at her, for she had mentioned my parents, and all through our conversation I had wondered who she reminded me of. She reminded me of my mother. Her charcoal-grey, big-eared Weimaraner pulled himself up on to the bench and nudged his way between us, taking it in turns to lick her face and then mine. Margaret – in her sixties, gentle, slim, pretty – chided him affectionately and he responded with more licks.

'My parents know exactly what I'm doing,' I said. 'So does my wife. I promise. There's no need to feel sorry for me. This is my choice.'

Finally putting the money back into her purse, Margaret instead insisted I take one of her apples, and that was a gift I could not refuse. She smiled sadly at me as if I brought someone to mind, and then rose from the bench. 'Archie, Archie, Archie!' she sang, and the dog flew from its seat and bounded off up and along the path in the direction of Hatherleigh. Margaret followed, turning once a minute to look back at me and wave.

I stayed in my seat, grateful for the rest. Margaret's outlook was rare – most believed my true story, but those that did not chose instead to see me as a menace. I had known that the latter would be the case through much of my journey. As far back as Elizabethan times, tramps – who in the sixteenth century were known as 'vagrants' or 'rogues' – were considered vermin or madmen, what Iain Sinclair calls the Tom O'Bedlams of their day. Under Tudor law, any vagrants who were caught were subjected to whipping, placement in the stocks, imprisonment, branding, or hanging. Those deemed fit to work were often sent against their will into slavery, deportation or forced labour in the galleys.

It held no account that many of these wandering 'rogues' were, in fact, either on the road in search of work for which they were well trained or on their way *to* work for which they were well trained. One case study from Warwick which dates back to the 1580s cites the arrest of 130 vagrants. Of these, seventy-seven were tradesmen or professionals on their way to or in search of their next job (and the remainder were mostly wives or children in tow). Almost a third were labourers and servants, then came cloth-workers, peddlers, tinkers, builders, a surgeon, a student, a mole-catcher, a coal-digger, a clockmaker, a roper, a locksmith and a barber. Nevertheless, most suffered corporal punishment for their tramping.

Tramps have been considered a problem for as long as recorded history will allow us to look back in time. In the year 1569 alone, around thirteen thousand 'rogues and masterless men' were arrested out of the approximate twenty thousand that existed across England. Only three years before, the Somerset Justice Edward Hext wrote that 'of these sort of wandering idle people there are three or four hundred in a shire', plus thirty to forty gypsies. We have the Elizabethans to thank for the coinage of that closing word: in those times, Romany gypsies were known as 'Egiptians'.

For all the public perception of vagrants, rogues and tramps throughout the ages, there is much evidence to suggest that they were never as problematic as their contemporary accounts made them out to be. What we might see in hindsight is instead that ancient antipathy which has existed between those who settle and those who choose to be nomadic, which has been recorded since the scriptures.

Bruce Chatwin, for whom nomadism was a poetic passion, traces the mutual distrust between nomads and settlers back to biblical times, when the nomads of Persia would look down upon their settled brothers with scorn at their childish need for the protections of cities and walls; and when the settled Egyptians would decry the Bedouin Hebrews as being akin to plagues of locusts, devouring their resources and then moving on to their next patch to do the same. Chatwin particularly notes the fallacy in the latter's thoughts: nomads do not wander aimlessly from each new ground to the next – in fact, most nomads move along their centuries-old tour or circuit of pastures in cyclical and repetitive patterns, allowing the ground to regenerate for when their families and cattle return months or years later. Indeed, the very word 'nomad' is derived from the Greek word *nomos*, which means 'pasture'.

Such antipathy, such distrust and such animosity continue to this day. There remains amongst our settlers a fundamental distrust of anyone who needs to move; and there also remains a deep dislike amongst our twenty-first century nomads of anyone who chooses to stay put.

5

Hatherleigh was one of those towns with a hill for a high street. I arrived in the early evening and walked to the top, where the peaks of Dartmoor capped the horizon. There was no one about. The shops had shut and the pubs did not seem to be open, either. If they were, their doors were closed, their windows were dark, and no noise came from within. I fancied I could unroll my sleeping bag in a beer garden and sleep undisturbed, but then two men, both in orange T-shirts and bald, appeared from a house to stand on its doorstep and smoke roll-ups. They stared at me as I passed, muttering something I could not hear. Tramps, I knew, would not be tolerated in small, provincial places like this, and anyway I was still not ready for sleeping on the streets just yet. No one really cared if you spent a night rough in the dunes or a cliff-side field, nor did they care if you were part of a city's homeless community (though they said they did to both cases). But in places like Hatherleigh, arrest was certain, and violence probable.

I had once wondered why there were so few homeless in the south-west and so many in places like London, Birmingham and Manchester. Why on earth did rough sleepers choose to hole themselves up in dirty cities on shop doorsteps when down here there were parks, rivers and beaches? One reason is money: cities are hives, and the more people who pass you on the street, the more likely they are to drop cash in your hat. But another reason is violence. The financial, retail and tourist areas of cities – where you are most likely to find rough sleepers – are protected by the police, who are bound by strict rules. Residential areas, on the other hand, are protected by the residents, men like these in Hatherleigh who have the territorial instinct to safeguard their land, their homes and their families from anyone alien and threatening, and who will slip around the law if they have to. These places are old, and they are bigoted.

I walked out and on to the main road – the A386, which connected Okehampton to Bideford – heading north in the vain hope that I would spot a likely sleeping-patch. It was still hours from sunset, but dark, pregnant clouds had floated over from Dartmoor, and the air was thick with the prospect of an early, rainy nightfall. There was no pavement on the A386 and few grass verges, and the occasional cars which passed me with their headlights on full-beam seemed to make no effort to swerve out from my hurried footsteps.

It was growing cold; I was growing hungry. To my side, a long, brambled hedgerow bisected the road and fields, some with cows, some with sheep, some with nothing at all. When the road was quiet, I scrambled over a hedge into an empty field, catching the frayed tips of my fingerless gloves on thorns, and then hid beneath it, out of sight of both the road and the farmhouse half a mile away. I cooked beans and ate them quickly. I needed to make some notes, but I was tired and a little scared, and so I climbed into my sleeping bag and fell asleep before eight o'clock.

I woke to a splashing downpour which had soaked my face and insinuated itself into my sleeping bag. The neck and shoulders of my T-shirt were dripping. I leapt out, pulled my poncho from my knapsack, and then squatted uncomfortably under it, waiting for the rain to stop. It got worse. I checked my watch. Three o'clock. The darkness and the sound of the rain were engulfing. I rolled my sleeping bag up and sat on it, extricated my towel from my knapsack, dried my face and torso as well as I could under my poncho, and placed it all back in the bin bag. I was just about dry now and my belongings were out of the rain, but I felt miserable. Three hours later, the torrent stopped, and I must have nodded off, for I awoke crumpled up on the ground to the noise of the morning rush-hour traffic, wet grass in my mouth.

6

Tired and irascible, I walked back into Hatherleigh to find it as quiet as the previous day, and this irritated me profoundly and irrationally. With little energy and less inclination to walk, I stood at the side of the road and stuck out my thumb.

Two hours later, a car slowed to a halt beside me. I stuck my head through the open door and asked, 'Where are you going?'

It is traditional for the driver, not the hitch-hiker, to ask this question, but I had no answer for it, except perhaps 'east', and this may have sounded suspicious.

'Tiverton,' the driver replied.

'Excellent,' I said, and got in.

He was a young man, perhaps twenty-five, with a friendly smile, but I was not in the mood for talking. When he asked what I did, I fed him the conversation-killer.

'I'm writing a book about walking from Land's End to London. I should really be walking now, but I had a bad night sleeping rough, so I'm cheating a bit by hitching.'

He seemed interested. 'Sleeping rough, eh? Why didn't you get a room for the night?'

'The book's about travelling and living like a tramp. I walk during the day and I sleep out at night. I don't have enough money on me to get a room. Last night I wished I did, though.'

'So it's like you're homeless.'

'More like a tramp.'

'Lot of homeless round my way,' he said, ignoring me. 'Thing I don't get is, they're all Eastern Europeans. Used to be, when I was a kid, they were British, but not any more. Don't get me wrong, I'm not racist or anything...' – that comment nearly always meant the opposite – '... and I've got nothing against the ones that come over here to work, even if they do undercut our tradesmen and put them out of business. But I don't think it's right to just come over here and abuse our benefits system.'

'Surely if they're homeless then they're not on benefits?'

'Selling *The Big Issue*, then.'

'That's not a benefit. That's a job.'

'So they're taking our jobs, then.'

'You just said you didn't mind that.'

He was quiet for a moment, and I thought I had offended him. But then he laughed. 'Yeah! I did, didn't I? Guess they can't be so bad, after all!'

I felt guilty for my hectoring tone. It was a rare man who did not resort to obstinacy when his ideas were challenged, and I liked him for being that rare man.

'So what you written, then?' he asked. 'Anything I might have read?'

I told him.

'Never heard of you.'

It was my turn to laugh. 'Not many people have.'

'Are you gonna hitch another lift from Tiverton or start walking again?'

'I should walk,' I said. It had begun to rain again, his car was warm and dry, and I could have happily curled up in its back seat and been driven all the way to London.

'Where to?'

'Wellington. If I stick to the road I should make it there by this evening.'

'If you're going to Wellington, you can walk most of the way along the Grand Western Canal. It's much nicer. I'll drop you off at the start. It's on the way into town.'

As he pulled up to the car park, I felt grateful to him, for he had given me good advice and then gone out of his way so that I could take it. I thanked him as I climbed out.

'No problem,' he said. 'Good luck with your book. And don't end up selling *The Big Issue* in London. I don't want to hear that you've been going up there, stealing their jobs.'

7

The so-called starting point of the Grand Western Canal was filled with boats and tourists. Swans hissed at curious dogs that rushed too close to the cygnets, and their owners laughed: '*He* just got told where to go.' Young families picnicked by the brown water and barges carried old couples in raincoats up and down the canal.

I walked east, pleased with the recommendation of this flat, gentle towpath. The boats decreased in number as the canal thinned, and for long miles I was alone tramping through quiet woodlands, the water at my side stagnant and topped with a foam of algae. I stopped for lunch – a Cup-a-Soup boiled in my mess tin and eaten with a spoon – in a clearing. The sun was at its peak overhead in a cloudless sky and I unfurled my sleeping bag on the towpath. It dried in minutes.

The plaques and leaflets in the unmanned Grand Western Canal Information Office had hinted that I could follow the canal all the way to Bridgwater, and I fancied that perhaps I should. But when I came out on the road at the small village of Holcombe Rogus to cross the Waytown Tunnel, I saw a sign for Wellington and remembered why I had wanted to stop there for the night.

My wife and I had once lived in Wellington and been bored there for over a year. I knew of a spot which would be perfect to spend the night, where it was safe and, most importantly, sheltered. With the memory of the previous night's misery resonating in my fatigued thighs, I left the canal and walked the 5 miles along a busy dual carriageway to the town, entering at the suburb of Rockwell Green with its Italianate water tower, where I had once driven past a man at midday lying in an unnatural position on a grass verge. I had stopped to ask if he was all right, and he had opened one eye and said, 'I am sleeping.'

I did not stop in Wellington, though I took a short detour to pass my old house, as one must, before making my way on to the road to the Wellington Monument. This 175-foot,

120-year-old plinth stands on the Blackdown Hills, leering down at the M5 motorway and, beyond it, the Vale of Taunton. Walking up the road which scaled the hill, a sign informed me that this was a 20 per cent gradient. After the Cornish coast path, I gloated at its easiness.

It used to be that you could sit with your back against the monument and admire the panorama, but when I arrived the stone had been fenced off with chicken wire, and the few gaps in the overgrown foliage offered measly vistas. Somewhere out there, not far to the west, was the Devon-Somerset border, which I must have crossed on the towpath, though no sign had marked it.

I had walked up here for what lay behind the monument: a stretch of navigable woodland with scores of places to unroll a sleeping bag beneath the cover of a domineering oak tree. It had those three things I had come to learn the tramp needs at night: safety, quiet and shelter. Sometimes older teenagers would drive up here for late-night sessions of drinking, smoking or shagging, or a combination of all three, but they rarely ventured from the seclusion of the monument. I knew I had a good spot here, and I was right, for I had the best night's sleep so far on the journey, woken only once when a rainstorm crashed into the tops of the trees above. I sat up and felt my sleeping bag and the ground. Both were dry. I fell back to sleep, smug.

8

Invigorated from my night in the woods, I set off before sunrise. I intended to get to Portishead, a fair distance, by the end of the day, for a bed waited there, and I could think of nothing more appealing. Walking back down the hill and through Wellington, I fell into step with three men from Lithuania on their way to work.

'What do you do?' I asked.

'We pick,' one replied.

'What do you pick?'

'Everything.'

The road from Wellington to Taunton was bordered by a pavement, which was fortunate, for I entered the latter with the morning rush-hour traffic and would have been terrified if I had been forced to step along the edge of the teeming road. At Taunton, I descended on to the Taunton-Bridgwater Canal: 15 miles of rabbits, faraway deer, motionless herons, and low, moss-covered bridges. Principally, it was duckland: hundreds of the birds swam back and forth and shrieked their laughing cackles. On the far side, the occasional head of a cat appeared slowly through the stems of corn, eyed the ducks and their safety in numbers, noted me, and then disappeared again.

The roar of the motorway was always near, and I walked under it more than once. Every half hour or so, I passed the carcass of a bird floating in the water. Each a different size and colour, they were all so brutally mangled as to render their species indistinguishable. I could not comprehend what had done this – perhaps a large pike patrolled these waters. Surely they had not been hit by the slow barges, becoming cousins to the gruesome roadkill I had seen throughout Devon. It began to rain, and large red puddles swelled along the path.

At Bridgwater I rose up through the town and walked to the motorway service station, where I stood at the exit with my thumb out. It was getting late and Portishead was too far away to make on foot by the end of the day. There were plenty of places to sleep around here, but I was determined to reach that bed.

'Where are you going, pal?' a white-van-man who called himself Milesy asked out of his window. I had let him ask first: I had an answer this time.

'Portishead.'

Milesy shook his head. 'I'm only going as far as Weston.'

'That'll do,' I said, and got in.

We came on to the M5 motorway directly into stationary traffic.

'You should have carried on walking, pal,' Milesy sighed.

At Weston-super-Mare I rejoined the coast path, walking over the hill to Sand Bay and then pushing on towards Clevedon. The sun was setting, and the lights of Cardiff and Newport began to twinkle across the Bristol Channel. An awkward farm protruded out, slicing through the path towards the impassable rocks, 'DO NOT ENTER' signs on its decaying fences. Grumbling and footsore, I took the long detour around it and back on to the path. From there, I knew it would take me all the way to Portishead and my friend's house, but I still had over an hour to go, the darkness was steadily building, and the path was overgrown so that the wet foliage brushing my boots with each step had finally permeated the waterproofing, and my feet were sodden. I strapped my miner's torch to my head and strode on.

It was ten o'clock by the time I reached the house. A large glass of wine was poured, and I fell asleep on the couch before touching it.

CHAPTER FOUR

BRISTOL STREETS

I

I spent the next two days housebound: sleeping and overeating and taking a bath a day with burgeoning agoraphobia. Portishead was another place I had lived for a few years, the familiarity bred comfort, and it was exactly what I needed. The rough sleeping thus far had been uncomfortable and it had been cold, but never had it been frightening. It would be soon, I knew. The tramp will spend nights in fields and dunes, on the fringes and in solitude, but he will also spend them on streets, inside the city walls and surrounded by peers. It was such peers who scared me the most. What would they make of me? What would they take?

On my final day, it occurred to me that I needed more money to see me through the rest of the journey to London. My original fifty pounds had dwindled with surprising rapidity – what had I used it for other than beans, bread, tea and water? – and, though there was still a full hundred sewn into my jacket, that was for emergencies, and I did not want to touch it. I walked to Portishead's branch of my bank.

It was an uncertain enterprise. I did not have my bank card. The cashier stared at me in disdain as I explained myself to her. I wished I had borrowed some of my friend's clothes. I wished I looked more respectable.

'Do you have any other ID?' she asked.

'No,' I said. 'But I know my sort code, my account number and any personal details you might need.'

Her fingers tapped across the keyboard between us, then moved to pluck a leaf of paper from its holder and pass it under the partition. 'Before we do anything, I need to see if your signature matches what we've got.'

I signed the paper and handed it back to her. She tapped at the keyboard again, read from the screen, tapped some more, and overall appeared very anxious. Two long minutes passed. The queue behind me was beginning to grow, and I could sense rising tempers, bored frustration.

'How long do you think…'

I was interrupted by a suited man who had appeared at my side without my noticing. 'Could you come with me, please, Mr Carroll?'

I looked back to the cashier, her anxiety melting into relief. 'Of course,' I said, and followed him through swing doors to a small alcove of an office in the rear of the building. As we sat opposite each other, he stared hard at me like a television detective, and I found it difficult to resist laughter.

'Why exactly do you not have your bank card with you, Mr Carroll?' he asked after a lengthy silence.

'I don't carry it everywhere,' I said.

'And what exactly do you need money for?'

'That's a very personal question,' I replied. 'One which I'm not going to answer.'

'You must understand that we rarely have customers entering the bank requesting money with absolutely no identification on them.'

I was growing tired of this faux interrogation from this overblown shopkeeper, who was perhaps at this moment imagining himself in a courtroom or holding-cell. My friend would lend me some money, I thought. 'I understand if you can't give me any money,' I said. 'But all you have to say is "no".'

'What's your full name?'

I told him.

'Your address with postcode?'

I told him.

'Your previous address with postcode?'

I told him.

'The address of your local branch? Your account number? Your sort code? Your three most recent purchases? How many direct debits do you have? How much do you pay for your mobile phone? How many credit cards do you have with us? What was the last deposit made in your account?'

I gave the correct answer to each until, exasperated, he finally said: 'All right. How much do you want?'

'Fifty pounds.'

'Fifty pounds?' His tone implied the question, *is that it?*

He left the office, returning moments later with my cash. I took it and stood up to leave. He looked baffled. I opened the door.

'Are you a mystery shopper?' he suddenly called out from behind me. 'Because if you are, you have to tell me.'

2

I left Portishead before dawn. I needed to get to Bristol by midday and spend the afternoon searching for an area where I could weather my first night on the streets with a small semblance of security. I knew the city well, but I knew it as a shopper or drinker, a day tripper: the homeless underbelly of Bristol was as alien to me as Tokyo, and I would have to learn it. Sadly, there was no guidebook for that.

A cycle-path took me from Portishead through the Gordano Valley and then alongside the Avon at Pill. I followed the river's low-tide sludge through woodland, along the base of the gorge and then beneath Brunel's suspension bridge. Dark, urban lanes criss-crossed out beneath the dual carriageway, swinging between abandoned warehouses with boarded-up windows and graffiti from 1983. Inexplicably, a pristine pop-up tent had been pitched beside the cycle-path which bordered this grimy hinterland. It must have been a cyclist's or hiker's – tramps and homeless did not have tents, I thought, and the kind of people who would frequent this place late at night did not *camp*. Little did I know that, not much later, I would find myself living in a tented community with other homeless upon London's streets.

My plan was to speak to any rough sleepers I could meet in Bristol and find out from them where I should sleep. Doubtless, there were unwritten rules I should be unaware of, and what I really wanted to know was where I should avoid. Perhaps there were areas where arrest was inevitable (on any private property), areas where kicks and taunts from passing locals were likely (outside any pub), or areas where the homeless themselves were the biggest threat. I was never so naive as to believe that all rough sleepers would welcome my attention or my presence – I knew that some were as volatile as fire, and a danger more to each other than to anyone else. Nevertheless, I hoped one or two might offer some advice. The homeless do not sleep down back alleyways in ten-strong cuddle-puddles like a litter of puppies, I was not going to be invited over to the nearest mattress, but they were still human, and I hoped the urge to help would shine through.

But Bristol, at first glance, seemed devoid of any kind of homeless life or activity. I checked my watch. It was not yet noon. *Perhaps it's too early*, I thought, then realised the absurdity of such an idea. The homeless didn't come out at a certain time of day. They were always out.

Crossing College Green, passing the Hippodrome and winding through the foamy water-features of Broad Quay, I came across no conspicuous rough sleepers. Passing me were throngs of university students; sitting on the benches were doting parents who watched their children splash in the jets and fountains; and walking towards me as I moved up Corn Street, of course, was a charity-hawker.

'Hello, Sir!' she beamed. 'You got a minute? I'm Nicky.'

'I don't think I can help you,' I replied. 'I don't have an address.'

Nicky smiled at me for a few moments more and, with cheerful thoughtlessness, said: 'But you're too clean to be a homeless.' The second the last syllable passed her lips, her eyebrows leapt up her forehead, her chin plummeted in the opposite direction, and her free hand clapped violently over her slack and hanging mouth. 'Oh my God,' she muttered between her fingers, 'I'm so sorry. I just... oh my God...' Locking her gaze on the ground, she hurried away.

At the top of the street I was accosted by another hawker. I stopped him before he could begin his pitch. 'I've already spoken to Nicky. Tell her I'm sorry I couldn't give her any money. At least I gave her an anecdote.'

The long shopping thoroughfare of Broadmead was similarly free of beggars, loiterers or street-drunks, and I began to despair that I would find no one to ask for advice. Contemplating the walk back to Portishead, I continued to trawl the streets, and finally found Sue selling *The Big Issue* near the university.

Sue was approaching middle age but already looked like a pensioner. She stood with a hunched stoop, giving the impression that her shoulders had set like plaster, and one of her legs shook with a faint but perceptible tremor. Though the sun was bright and reaching its peak, Sue wore the hood of her red vendor-jacket pulled in tight so no hair or neck was visible, only the poked-out extremities of her bird-like face. But it was a face which never stopped smiling, which spoke only happy words, and which laughed as a punctuation marker every few seconds: a face I found lovely.

There was a two-pound coin in my wallet and I bought a copy of *The Big Issue*. Sue thanked me profusely in her round, rolling Bristolian accent, and we fell to talking. I asked how long she had been homeless.

'Oh, years, my love, years. But *technically*, I'm not actually homeless any more. Haven't slept rough for nearly seven months now.' She announced the last sentence with undisguised pride. 'Nope, I been living in this flat looking after this bloke – lovely guy, he is. He retired a few years ago, and he's got some kidney problems, so what I do is I cook for him and clean the flat and do all the shopping, and he lets me live there for nothing.'

I pointed at the magazine in my hand. 'Are you still allowed to sell this if you've got a place?'

She giggled. 'I know, bit cheeky, innit? But, nah, it's all right, I've cleared it. See, I've got a place but I ain't got no money, so I need to keep selling this for just a little longer until I gets a job. But that'll be coming soon, too. I've got me place, I'm sorting things out with me husband – next stop, a job. Can't bloody wait. Life is good.'

Another customer bought a magazine: after dropping the two pound coins into Sue's gloved hand he smiled awkwardly at me and then walked away. 'Thank you, my love!' Sue called after him. 'You have a cracking day!'

'So,' I faltered, suddenly nervous at the question I was about to ask. I was nervous because I reasoned Sue would ask me my status, and I did not want to lie; or perhaps she would just see right through me, and then I would lie out of misguided panic. 'Where's decent to sleep around here?'

Sue asked no questions, and barely even looked at me as she fired off a response so quick it seemed automatic. 'Couldn't really say,' she replied with no succeeding justification. Another customer approached her.

'Of course, my love, thank you so much. You look after yourself,' Sue said as she handed over the magazine, and then, as her customer left, turned to me and grinned: 'What a day!'

'What about where you used to sleep?' I persisted.

'Nah, can't stop there any more. Closed off. It changes all the time. I don't really know any more.' Again that swift delivery, that mechanical and almost rehearsed answer which gave nothing away. It was so unlike the candour of her earlier confessions, and one of the few things she said to me not delivered with a smile.

I continued walking, away from the centre and towards Stokes Croft. At the underpass by the bus station, a busker hollered an incomprehensible song, and I leaned against a wall and waited for him to finish. His leather jacket hung in tattered strands from his shoulders and the spikes of his Mohawk were wilted and grey. It was this cavern of the underpass which stank of piss, but it looked like it could have been him. He moved arhythmically between a D and a G chord, bellowing gibberish above the out-of-tune triads. He had made £1.20. Finally, he came to the end of his song and nodded at me. I approached him.

'All right, pal?' he asked.

'Do you know anywhere round here to sleep?' I asked, favouring a direct approach.

'Ha! Nah, I ain't getting into that.' He paused. 'You got a guitar tuner?'

'No.'

'Ah, well.' And with that he burst sonorously into the next song, an atonal note for atonal note replica of its predecessor.

Along Gloucester Road, an old man with a beard which crawled up his cheeks towards his eyebrows rummaged through the ashtrays of a pub's roadside beer garden, carefully placing the choicest morsels in his pocket. When he saw me watching, he smiled and held one out to me. I took it.

'No light, though,' he said, and I handed it back. 'What are you?' he asked, casting a long gaze down my body to observe my clothes. They still looked cheap and ragged, but I had cleaned them, and myself, thoroughly in Portishead. 'Outreach?'

I shook my head. Again, I was uncomfortable lying. I did not want to say 'I'm homeless', because I wasn't, and to say 'I'm a tramp' somehow sounded ludicrous. 'I'm walking,' I said.

He seemed happy with that, and continued to forage in an ashtray.

'I was wondering if you could help me out,' I said. 'Whereabouts can you sleep round here?'

'I'm not going to get into that,' he said, stepping backwards. 'I'm not going to get into that.'

Those words again. What was it with Bristol's homeless? All had been kind to me in their own way – Sue's cheerful intimacy, the guitarist's encouraging nod, this tramp's proffered stub of a smoked cigarette – but when my stock question came up this sudden evasion and concurrent suspicion was unanimous. Why did they think I was asking? This latter man believed I worked for Outreach – an organisation which supports people with learning difficulties or mental health needs. Perhaps the others did, too. Or, worse, perhaps they thought I worked for the council or the police, here to uncover the local pockets of rough sleepers and move them off Bristol's streets. Perhaps even they mistook my question for an invitation – 'Want to share my sleeping bag?' – and the response 'I'm not going to get into that' was far more literal than I had understood. Most likely, I thought, they simply had a tried and tested spot, one which was safe and dry, quiet even, and revealing its location to a stranger would be the equivalent of giving that stranger your door keys.

I rolled those adjectives around my mind: safe, dry, quiet. A stretch of woods flanked the edge of the Avon before the gorge – I had registered them as I passed on the way into the city that morning. It was an unplanned but unavoidable consequence of becoming a tramp: I looked for and assessed likely sleeping-spots everywhere. Those woods, I noticed, were littered with beer cans and cigarette or condom packets on the periphery, but inside they were dense enough to hide a quiet individual. The thought appealed to me. It was not late, but I was tired and I was hungry, and the woods were only a half-hour walk from the centre. I bought a tin of beans and a loaf of bread from a supermarket and set off for them.

3

Four large trees with low-hanging branches and thick clusters of leaves sheltered an inner quadrangle. Inside, the treetops arched inwards to form a tangled and spiny cone, and there was enough room to hang a hammock, if only I had brought one along. This was my nest. Each evening, I came back from the centre and slept here. The nights grew colder, but little rain ever fell inside the quadrangle, and the walls of leaves deflected the winds. Though I often cut myself as I pushed through the sharp and splayed branches to exit or enter, once inside I felt secure and comfortable. I cooked there, slept there and, when it was light enough, could even perch on one of the tree's branches with my back against the trunk to happily read my book. Often, after it was dark and I was wrapped within my sleeping bag, noises floated across from the outer edges of the woods – laughter, shouting, singing, grunts, hoots, shrieks, and once, on a weekend night, the splintering crash of broken glass followed by a howl – but such noises were never close enough to cause concern. My little woodland den became both refuge and relief.

It was early when I walked back into Bristol following my first night in the woods. I was beginning to enjoy living by the rise and set of the sun: it felt natural and elemental, and I was free of the mild guilt which always succeeded a late night and a lie-in. At the same time, I knew my joy was seasonal, and I would feel very different when, not long from now, daylight only lasted for eight of each twenty-four hours.

In the centre, the shops were still closed. A thin mist hung along the streets of Broadmead. A man sat with his back against a wall, sipping slowly from a can of ale. I recognised the brand. It was not cheap.

'Where's good to—'

'Fuck off,' he growled.

4

I met Jan on a bench at Broad Quay. He was dressed warm, had a thick Polish accent, a wide grin and the peach-fuzz stubble of a schoolboy. 'I haven't seen you in Bristol before,' he said.

'I'm new to the area.'

'Have you been to The Wild Goose yet?'

'No.'

'Oh-holy-shit-Jesus-Christ-motherfucker!' he cried, spewing the words out as if they were a single, monosyllabic obscenity. 'You haven't been to The Wild Goose? You must! You must!'

'What is it?'

'It is the best place in the world. Run by the best people in the world. You can get food there, food for free. Do you know Easton? Stapleford Road? Just head for the swimming pool. It is close to this. If you go now, you might be in time for the end of breakfast.'

'Thanks,' I said, rising to go. 'You coming?'

Jan shook his head. 'Already eat. Today will be a good day for business, so I must make an early start.'

'What's your business?'

'What do you think?' Jan laughed, pulling his vendor-jacket and a stack of *Big Issue*s from his bag. I thanked him again and walked away in search of Easton and The Wild Goose. Jan stopped me a few steps later with a shout. 'Charlie!' he called. 'Oh-holy-shit-Jesus-Christ-motherfucker, you are going the wrong way!' He pointed in the opposite direction, and I set off again.

I was too late for breakfast, so passed the hours before The Wild Goose reopened for lunch by wandering Easton. It was a bleak part of the Greater Bristol metropolis, the poorer cousin to the city centre and the more affluent areas such as Clifton and Redland. Down one backstreet, legal notices were affixed to doors, warning any squatters who might be there that they *would* be evicted. Down another, alternate houses had replaced the glass in their ground-floor windows with sheets of plywood. Along the main street, a sign hung from the door of a small and independent shop begging passers-by to refrain from destroying the flowerbox which sat on the windowsill. The sign seemed to have worked, for the flowerbox was intact and in bloom, and it was the prettiest thing on the street.

The morning passed slowly. I checked my watch with frequent impatience, waiting for the doors of The Wild Goose to open. When they finally did, I was less than two minutes late. Already, the place bustled with life.

The best place in the world, run by the best people in the world. Those were Jan's words, and he was right. The Wild Goose is a wonderful, generous, altruistic, kind, magnificent, philanthropic and gladdening institution, open to all. The owner, Alan Goddard, once said, 'It doesn't matter if you have one pound in your pocket or one million. You are welcome to eat here.' They served free food to anyone who entered, and all they asked in return was that nobody smoked, took drugs or fought either on the premises or outside of it. Such rules were adhered to by all.

The crowd that afternoon was varied and plentiful. Only one was obviously homeless: an old man with a thin, white beard and rips in his woollen jumper which revealed further rips in the woollen jumper he wore beneath it. I caught him staring at me each time I looked over from my beans on toast, shovelled up with a plastic knife and fork. When our eyes met, his instantly darted to the floor, though whether it was from fear, shame or embarrassment, I could not decipher.

Around the edges of the room, single men sat and focused on their food: most young and tattooed, others with shirts and brushed hair, all seemingly red-eyed and exhausted. In the middle, the largest table was occupied by four teenage girls who loudly boasted about the number of care homes they had been through, boyfriends in jail who hadn't written for two weeks, how many blokes Lisa had shagged last week – 'she's already got warts, she'll get chlamydia next, the fucking skank' – and why lager had a better buzz than cider. One rapped a verse so rapid it was incomprehensible, another cupped her hands around her lips and beatboxed, and a third rose from her seat, leaned her elbows on the table and wiggled her arse furiously at the two Eastern Europeans eating their slices of sponge cake.

I turned away from the spectacle to see a large man huff through the door.

'Stan!' the young lady serving behind the counter called as he approached. She piled beans on toast (a far larger portion than she had given me) on to a plate and thrust it towards him. 'All right, gorgeous?'

'Hullo, my pretty,' Stan replied, letting his eyes trail from her blonde hair to her glasses to the spiderweb of tattoos along her arm.

He took a seat at my table and nodded to me.

'You must be a regular,' I said.

'Came here for the first time yesterday,' he replied, and winked at me. I knew then that I was in the presence of a charming old bastard.

5

Stan was the only person I met on that long walk from Sennen to London who called himself a tramp. The pockets of his faded green puffa jacket were stuffed with small, plastic cola bottles: most empty, but some filled with cheap vodka. I had some once and it nearly blinded me. Stan's nose and cheeks were a grid of burst capillaries, his eyes bulged out as if someone had squeezed him too hard, he had the wrinkles of a lifetime smoker and the dental hygiene of an aged camel, but he managed to have a wet shave and flatten his thick hair down with Brylcreem once a day. He made a point of that.

'Why won't anyone tell me where I should sleep?' I asked him as we left The Wild Goose together.

'Why should they?'

'I'm not asking where *they* sleep, I'm asking for any spot.'

'There's plenty of good sleeping-spots in Bristol, but we don't just stick to one, we move around. Me, I've got about five, I know another ruddy *ten*, but I wouldn't tell you about them, either.'

'Why not?'

'What if I need them myself?' He stopped on the pavement and turned to face me. His palm bounced off the spring of his hair as he absent-mindedly checked for consistency. 'All right, then, Charlie, tell me this. Where did *you* sleep last night?'

I visualised my den, from the dry sleeping bag unfurled on the soft ground to the spire of interlocked branches at its peak. I was not prepared to reveal it to anyone. 'Good point,' I said.

Stan laughed. I do not believe I had ever seen anyone so pleased with themselves. 'Come on. Let's go to Castle Park. I need some baccy and there's a guy there who sells it cheap.'

The image of the archetypal tramp paints him as alone. In fact, this is not the case. When you see homeless on their own, they are more often than not new to the streets. Humans are inherently social animals, and the need to pack is one of our most primitive urges. Though so much else of what we might consider included in being human is stripped from the homeless, this instinct is not, and the whole gamut of social relationships – from the casual acquaintance to the close circle to the best friend – exists as profoundly amongst the homeless as it does amongst the homed.

By Bristol, I was no longer new to rough sleeping, but I was new to the streets, and that, coupled with the hostility I had felt so far, pushed me into keeping myself to myself. So Stan was a welcome ray of light. We met each day and, for the short time I stayed in Bristol, we became friends. Eating with him at The Wild Goose, sitting together under the covered arches of Cabot Circus when it rained, accepting free mugs of tea at a Methodist chapel and politely nodding along to the evangelising of our hosts, and sharing his vodka and my cans of lager at Castle Park in the evenings, his company cheered me, and I think mine cheered him, too.

'This book you're writing,' he said, for I had told him the truth regarding my journey, 'am I going to be in it?'

'I hope so. Do you mind?'

'You'll have to speak to my lawyer.'

I needn't have worried along the Cornish coast of thinking up a back-story. Stan accepted my reasons for rough sleeping as naturally as if I had told him any plausible tales of addiction and downward spirals. He spoke often about his own time on the streets over the years, but only once, during our last night together, did he allude to what originally put him there. Stan's verbose nostalgia was a rarity on the streets – I came to learn that most homeless did not talk about their past, often because they did not want to. For 99 per cent of homeless people in England, the past will hold shame; shame which is best left alone. Few homeless talk about the future, either. Theirs is instead the present, in itself absorbing enough.

6

I felt nervous. The door was locked. There was a buzzer and intercom system: an explanation was demanded before entry allowed. Four young men with cigarettes, tracksuits and welts on their faces hovered near the door, and I became so paranoid that my voice would betray me I had to leave and walk around the block. The men watched me leave and return minutes later. I prayed I had the courage to try my hand or – more accurately – my accent.

'Hello?' A distorted voice through a tinny waist-high speaker.

I bent down and kept my voice low. 'I just wanted to talk to someone.'

'Are you sleeping rough?'

The voice had not asked if I was homeless. To answer 'yes' would be to tell the truth. I *was* sleeping rough, but here it suddenly all seemed like a silly folly, and I could not bring myself to admit it. That morning, I had visited a Bristol City Council office to enquire about provisions for the homeless, and had been referred here: the Compass Centre. A combination of hostel, Outreach centre, health service and advice bureau, the Compass Centre was Bristol's flagship in care for the homeless and destitute. If I admitted over that intercom that I was sleeping rough, they might insist I take a bed for the night, and I could not do that. There was a bed only a few miles away in Portishead if I needed it, and the thought of a legitimate rough sleeper missing out on a hostel bed for the night because of me and my research appalled me.

'No,' I replied.

'I don't think there's anyone who can see you right now. Are you staying somewhere?'

'A friend's,' I said.

'Hold on a minute.' Murmurs percolated through the intercom, and I heard '... anyone available... guy here... sleeping on his mate's sofa'. Those last words had been assumed, I never said 'sofa', but it was a testament to the kind of problems people came here with. The voice returned. 'I might be able to get someone to see you. Pull the door on the buzz.'

Feeling the stares of the young men behind me on my back and the smoke of their cigarettes around my bare ears, I pulled on the door.

Inside it was warm, clean and calm as heaven. Clutches of men and women stood in same-sex groups yapping happily over cups of tea. Three young women with greasy hair scraped brutally back from their foreheads looked me up and down brazenly, five men behind them maintained a conversation without taking their eyes off the women, and a group of tall Eastern Europeans leaned over a banister, pulling up the sleeves of their knitted sweatshirts and scratching at their stubble. One raised his mug to me and smiled. Behind them, visible through floor-to-ceiling windows was the smoking area, and the dozen or so who puffed out there leaned out of the way of the towering plants in the centre, careful not to disturb them. The thought of unrolling my sleeping bag in a corner and falling into a slumber was overwhelming.

'I'm sorry, mate,' the man at reception said, brushing away the thick hair which hung over his eyes. 'No one can see you right now. Thought they might, but...'

'It's all right,' I said.

'Rough sleeping's our priority.'

'It has to be,' I agreed.

'Here,' he said, unfolding a grainy, photocopied map on to the counter and circling a street with a fluorescent yellow marker. 'Go to Phoenix Court. It's the Bristol City Council office. If you're not rough sleeping now but think you might end up having to, they can help you.'

I decided not to tell him I had already been there, that they had been the ones who sent me here. I was aware that the few short moments he had talked with me would have been better spent with someone in genuine need, and I did not want to waste any more of his time. Instead, I thanked him shyly, and left.

Outside, descending the steps, I was seized by horror. The man walking along the pavement on the other side of the road was, I realised, someone I had been to college with. I could not remember his name and was sure he would not remember mine, but if I had recognised his face then doubtless such identification would be reciprocated. Pulling my hood over my cap, I pointed my eyes at the ground and walked in the opposite direction. We were not acquainted enough to acknowledge each other, but if he placed me, coupled that with my garb and then clocked the nature of the building I was exiting, there was a chance he might remark on it to someone, perhaps someone I knew. The unbearable shame of homelessness hit me at that moment, and I wasn't even homeless.

7

I told Stan about my visit to the Compass Centre.

'Hundreds – no – ruddy *thousands* of places like that across the country,' he said. 'Some are pits, and I'm talking pits of ruddy *hell*, but some are spot on.'

I described the Compass Centre to him.

'Sounds nice,' he remarked wistfully.

'Why don't you try and get in there? If I was for real, I would.'

Stan looked at me for a moment. 'Because I don't want to,' he said simply. 'I'm off for a kip. I'll see you later, Charlie, yeah?'

When we met up again that afternoon, Stan, half-drunk, revealed his theory of homelessness. 'Anyone can get out of homelessness,' he said between sips of his vodka. 'No matter how deep in they are. They just have to want to. That's the main problem. Most people don't ruddy *want* to.'

He, for one, did not, as he categorically explained. 'I could be living a normal life right now. But I've chosen this.' The issue, he said, was that he was deeply addicted to vodka and cigarettes. Every evening he drank vodka and smoked cigarettes until he passed out. 'That's what I do. That's how my life is. That's how I *want* my life to be. I've tried it all, but I've never attained such contentment as those two beauties give me. Anyway, I'm fifty-one now, my heart, liver and lungs are all fucked, so what's left for me?'

Stan was certain he would not see sixty. He had left it too late. Never married, never had kids. All his family were dead. 'The Crushaw line stops with me. It's no big deal.'

'I don't think I could do this year-round,' I said. 'Sleeping rough now is barely tolerable, and it's only just autumn. I couldn't handle the winter.'

'Doesn't bother me. I run hot.' He stubbed his cigarette into the grass and lit another. 'I suppose I wouldn't mind a little flat or something, but when you're homeless you can't just get your own place as easy as that. You have to go through a whole process, shelters, refuges, flatshares, all that bollocks. And there's no way I'd survive all that, not the level I'm at. You see, in most of these halfway houses you can't drink, and you definitely can't smoke. Some have a curfew, all doors locked at nine o'clock. What if I'm still awake and need a drink or a fag? No. I can't be doing with that.'

Stan's words echoed with an idea which had been building in my mind for some time. Already, I had seen some of the provisions in place for rough sleepers in the UK, and I had been surprised that they were not more successful. But the issue of homelessness was not so black and white as I had imagined before beginning my journey. Many rough sleepers, like Stan, were still on the street because they believed it was the best option for them.

While few ever chose homelessness the first time round, some rough sleepers who have been rehabilitated, put through schemes and systems, placed in housing and hooked up with a secure, albeit minimum-wage, job, have chosen to jack it all in and return to the streets. It is a kind of reversed institutionalism. Living on the streets is not easy, but if done for long enough it can become normal, and any departure from normality is difficult for most. Some theories claim that it can take just four weeks for a person to assimilate to street life and, more importantly, the street community. And, if you begin to develop a stronger relationship with this community than with your previous peers – if, for example, your homelessness was the outcome of escape from an abusive relationship – the prospect of returning to 'normal' life can be more disheartening than staying on the streets.

Stuart Shorter, the eponymous hero of Alexander Masters' biography *Stuart: A Life Backwards*, often referred to homelessness as self-destruction: a quality anyone who has spent any time on the streets will tell you is rife amongst the homeless. Many feel not just that they *have* to live on the streets, but indeed that they *deserve* to, as if they are not good enough for rehousing, rehabilitation, reintegration.

'I'm perfectly happy,' Stan continued, 'lying in my sleeping bag, drinking my vodka and smoking my tobacco until I'm tired enough to sleep. If someone's there to chat to, that's a welcome bonus, but I enjoy my own company. And anyway, my two best friends are company enough.'

Stan still had rules, though. He would not start drinking before three o'clock in the afternoon: he refused to do it all day long, making sure to preserve it as a night-time pursuit. He kept it that way because, as he said, if it was perpetual there would be no pleasure. 'Get something all the time and it loses its fun. That hour, between two and three, that's my favourite hour of the day. I know what's coming.'

It was now only five o'clock, and already his eyes had grown rheumy and his speech slurred. It was sometimes like this. Most days, Stan could drink for a solid ten hours; other days, two cigarettes and a mouthful of vodka would knock him to his back, and from the floor he would gently sing early U2 songs.

I was not in the mood for drinking myself, and the afternoon was still warm, so I left Stan and walked the Zig Zag pathway up to Clifton, where I sat on the Downs, cooked dinner on my stove, and lay back to enjoy the setting sun.

Four students – two boys, two girls – approached. One of the boys, perhaps trying to impress his female companions, took his wallet from his pocket and sidled close to me. I had made a resolution early on to accept money from no one and, if it was forced on me, to pass it on to a homeless person. The boy came so close his shoulders blocked the sun, and I considered how to politely refuse his charity.

'Knock, knock,' he said.

'Who's there?' I replied.

'I thought you were meant to be homeless?' He laughed, tucked the wallet back into his jeans, and turned to one of the girls. She joyously shrieked at him, 'OMG! Did you really just do that?' and the four sauntered away together in a fog of guffaws and chortles.

Never have I wanted so much to punch a man in the mouth.

8

Dinner at The Wild Goose was soft pasta topped by a ladle of tomato sauce. I fancied I could taste garlic. Cubes of a crunchy and unidentifiable substance – perhaps undercooked potato, perhaps a soya-based meat substitute – permeated each mouthful. Stan had not arrived, but this was half-expected. It was already eight o'clock, and he would doubtless be tucking into his own liquid dinner.

I sat alone as I cleared my plate. Two Eastern Europeans shared my table, but their common language designated me as an outsider. A woman – short, in her forties, too much lipstick – joined the table and sat on the chair which faced mine. She dabbed at her pasta with a slice of bread, chewed twice, and then stared at me.

'Hello,' I said, uncomfortable under the gaze.

'What's your name? I'm Tanya.' I could not place her accent: a mixture of the Home Counties and Scotland, with some Mediterranean thrown into the vowels.

'Nice to meet you, Tanya,' I replied, holding my hand over the plates for her to shake gingerly. 'I'm Charlie.'

'I've seen you here before.'

'I haven't seen you.'

'Didn't we have a little chat the other night?'

'Definitely not. I would have remembered.'

'I'm sure of it. You're Charlie, aren't you?'

'I've just told you that.'

'You've told me it before.'

'No, Tanya,' I remonstrated. 'I haven't.'

'Yes, you have,' she persisted. 'Now I think of it, it wasn't here. We met at that party in St Paul's last week. You brought your dog. What was he called? Brian? Brice? Something like that.'

Relief replaced trepidation. This wasn't clumsy flirtation: Tanya had mistaken me for someone else. I explained I had not set foot in St Paul's for at least a year, and she seemed to accept the mistake.

'Then who the fuck *did* I meet?' she laughed.

A man approached and crouched down next to Tanya, his forearms crossed on the table. He was my age, with a thin face and dark, greasy hair. Tattoos trailed across his arms, but they were so faded I could not decipher what they symbolised. A twitch around the left eye became pronounced as he looked at me, and then faded again when he turned back to Tanya.

'You want to go?' he asked her.

'You got it?' she replied.

'Of course.'

Tanya rose from her seat, her pasta barely touched. 'Nice to meet you, Charlie,' she said, then began an awkward march towards the door. I watched her leave, noticing that her strange walk came from the high heels which, a size too large, inched away from her feet with each step. The man followed her, hands in pockets, eyes on the ground. Beside me, the two Eastern Europeans chuckled while one placed his hands – palms up, fingers curved as if clutching balloons – before his chest, jiggled them, and then squeezed air.

9

I did not see Stan for the next few days. Bristol was boring without him, and I considered leaving. It was about time anyway. I was looking forward to walking again, along the towpaths to London. But then he turned up for lunch at The Wild Goose one day, and my departure plans crumbled.

'I thought you might have left,' I said.

'Left? I only just got here. No. Just had to shoot off for a few days. Needed to make a bit of money.'

'What were you doing?'

Stan looked at me and smiled. 'There are some things, Charlie,' he said, 'that I don't want going in your book.'

But there were many other things which he did not mind about at all. Stan did not talk about the days before he became homeless – everything before the age of forty was excluded – but all that had occurred over the last ten years was fair game, confirmed by the frequent imperative, 'Put *that* in your book'.

Like the tramps of *Down and Out in Paris and London*, of *As I Walked Out One Midsummer Morning*, of those gloomy and monochrome inter-war years, Stan toured the country. Before Bristol, where he had been living only for the last month or so, he had spent time in Chester, Leeds, London, Bournemouth, Worcester, Northampton and Newcastle. Some places he stayed for months, others for years. Some places he left through choice, others because he had to. Every place, it seemed, had a story. Bournemouth, for example, was not its beach nor its sleeping-spots nor its climate, but was 'where I saved that kid'.

I pictured Stan on the beach at the peak of the summer, fully clothed and drunk while those around with their exposed and tanning flesh did their best to avoid eye contact with the filthy tramp; there is a scream – a small child has been caught in a rip current and is being carried out to sea; Stan, fuelled with alcohol, leaps in, thrashes towards the youngling, scoops him up in glistening, tattooed arms, and carries him back to shore; as one, the beach comes together to surround Stan, hoist him into the air cheering, and carry him to the nearest strip club with fresh wads of twenties bursting from his pockets.

I told him that. He laughed and said, 'Where do you ruddy *live*, Charlie?' Stan's life was never so easy, nor so light. 'I saved the kid from being raped.'

Bournemouth, Stan explained, had a disproportionately high population of rough sleepers. 'It's got a lot going for it, that place, so a lot of homeless turn up and then stay. I liked it there. Weather wasn't too bad – not for me, anyway, I'd just come down from ruddy *Newcastle* – and there's always a load of tourists around to scrounge from. Best of all, though, is there's loads of parks there, and no one comes to check them at night, so there's plenty of action. But you've got to have your wits about you if you're going to hang around those parks after dark. And that kid didn't.'

Stan's 'kid' was not the helpless toddler I had imagined – he was a gay eighteen-year-old who had an unfortunate habit of getting drunk in a nearby nightclub and then turning up at the wrong end of the park trying to pick up.

'There's places he could have gone for that. Safe places. But he kept coming back to the park, and he wasn't subtle either. He'd walk through shouting at the top of his voice what he wanted and how. Nobody paid him much mind at first. But then I heard that three blokes were starting to talk about him. And these were not nice blokes.'

Nor were they Stan's friends. He did not mix with them, but they shared mutual acquaintances. One – Stan would not tell me his name – revealed to Stan that the three men were planning on giving the young lad 'what he wanted' that night. He was going to watch; did Stan want to join him?

'I knew that meant they were going to rape him. And at first I didn't care too much. Maybe it was what he wanted. He used to shout some pretty rough things. I wasn't going to watch, but I wasn't going to try and stop it, either. None of my business. But then this other guy told me something I didn't know. One of those blokes was HIV.'

By Stan's logic, the best method of intervention was attack. He could not attack the three men, each of them alone was tougher than him, so he decided to attack the boy.

'I got him the moment he set foot in the park. He always came in the same way, and usually at the same time, so I knew where and when. The other three were somewhere deeper, hiding, waiting to ambush, so I had to get to him first. I nutted him hard enough so that he could feel it through the drink and told him that if he ever came into this park again I'd cut his feet off.'

'Did he?'

'Not as far as I know. I stayed around for the next two weeks and he never came back then. But I had to go after that.

I wasn't in danger or anything. Everyone knew what I'd done and why, and no one gave a shit, not even the three blokes. But I stopped liking Bournemouth after that. It lost its fun.'

London, too, was little more than a setting for Stan's only love story.

'See,' he said, 'most people think all us tramps are single. Not the case. Not the case *at all*. I know plenty in healthy and stable relationships. But if you want a woman you've got to head to the big cities, the bigger the better. And there's no bigger or better than London.'

'So why's that?' I asked. 'Are there more female rough sleepers there?'

'Just more ruddy *women*, Charlie. They don't have to be on the streets. My Melissa wasn't.'

I found this hard to believe, and my incredulity must have shown.

'Rapists and murderers have girlfriends, why can't I? You'd be surprised how many guys on the streets have girlfriends with houses and jobs tucked away here and there – and some of those girlfriends aren't that close to the breadline, if you know what I mean. Look, when you get to my age, you're as libido-less as a neutered dog. I haven't had a hard-on for three years. But all those younger ones – more and more of them every day, if you ask me – are as randy as a young man *should* be, and they've got to get some somewhere. There's a few women on the streets, but not enough to keep things fair.'

Melissa was considerably younger than Stan: in her late thirties while he had passed his mid forties. Her three children were all in care, she had finally divorced her husband after years of abuse, and she lived alone in a small bedsit south of the Thames.

'She had the most beautiful face,' Stan said. 'I mean, stunning, really stunning. Honestly, Charlie, if you saw her you would have fancied her. Like a model. But when you saw her body, that was when you realised what that cunt had done to her, and you forgot about her face. Scars and burns all over. And really bad ones, too, ones you could tell came from a knife. Her right arm was completely disfigured from the shoulder to the elbow, absolutely mashed, because he had taken a fucking blowtorch to her.'

Stan first met Melissa in a church: they were both there for the free tea. Usually, Stan preferred to juggle his charitable institutions for the sake of variety, but he kept returning to that church each day in the hope of seeing Melissa again. A week later, she reappeared, and Stan convinced her to join him for a drink in the park. She agreed, but it was mid February, and as they sat together on a bench she shivered so hard she could barely speak. The next week, she invited him back to her bedsit. At first, he declined, but then she told him he could drink and smoke there, and Stan moved in for the next eight months.

'I really loved her, you know,' he said. 'Still do. Never had anyone like that in my life, before or since. But in the end I had to go. We weren't...' he paused and searched for the word, '... compatible.'

He rubbed his eyes and fell quiet. I wanted him to continue, but I had not seen him look so fragile before. Five minutes passed before he spoke again.

'When she was drunk, she was ruddy *mental*.' He breathed in deep and then exhaled with a hissing sigh. 'Completely nuts.

One minute in hysterics on the floor crying over her kids, the next threatening to chop my balls off if I didn't give her another one, then suicidal, then hitting me, then hitting herself. It was like it flicked a switch in her, and there was nothing I could do except wait it out until she fell asleep and then woke up sober again. And when she was sober she was adorable, *that* was when I loved her. But she drank every night.'

'Had she always been an alcoholic?'

'No! That was the problem. *She* wasn't the alcoholic, *I* was! And how's she supposed to not drink when I start at three o'clock on the dot every day!'

'Jesus, Stan...' I muttered.

'What?'

'Why didn't you just stop fucking drinking? Just for once?'

I thought for a moment he might hit me, but instead he flicked his cigarette across the park, stood up, growled, 'Go fuck yourself, Charlie,' and then strode away.

10

I missed breakfast at The Wild Goose, and Stan was not there for lunch, but I found him in his usual spot in the park at three o'clock and sat next to him. He nodded and passed me a bottle of vodka. I took a swig and passed it back. Neither of us was sorry for what we had said the night before, but we let it pass, and the brief spell of awkwardness soon dissipated. Stan did not, however, mention Melissa to me again.

I bought a pack of beers from the nearby supermarket and the both of us set about getting drunk. I enjoyed the slow slip into inebriation out here in public, the growing warmth, the loosening of muscles, the descent from concern to indifference of what passers-by must think. 'Sod 'em!' Stan slurred, and stumbled off to piss in the river. Dusk and then night-time settled. Everything got funnier. A police car kerb-crawled along the road behind us, slowing to a stop, and we grabbed our plastic bags and sprinted off to find a quieter spot, giggling with excitement. The movement felt good and we continued to walk, the street lights becoming kaleidoscopic, our feet tripping and hopping. Sometimes we collapsed behind bins or leaned back against shop windowpanes, but mostly we moved. We could not go to The Wild Goose for dinner. We were too drunk to enter. We were too drunk to find it.

It was growing late; I usually liked to be asleep in my den by this hour. But the alcohol made me both fearless and energetic, and as I stomped along beside Stan, now in full storytelling mode, I thought perhaps that he was the best friend I had ever had.

'Did I tell you about Worcester, where I saw a guy eat dog-shit for money...'

'Then there was Northampton and the door-to-door salesman...'

'How about Bournemouth, where I saved that kid...'

We arrived at a tall and crumbling house. Next to it, set back somewhat, was an open garage and, inside that, a large and dirty sofa covered with a sleeping bag. The garage stank of stale cigarette smoke. 'Student house,' Stan said. 'Or, at least, I think it is. All the rest on this street are. But this one's empty. I tried to get in, it's locked up too tight, but this garage is always open. It's all right, eh?'

Stan had taken me to his sleeping-spot. We *were* best friends.

'Feel free to kip on the floor if you want. Couch is mine. I'm fucked.' He rolled himself into his sleeping bag. I sat on the floor and opened my last can of beer. It was dark in the garage, and Stan's face appeared in a jaundiced glow each time he puffed on his cigarette.

'Leeds,' he muttered. 'Have I told you about Leeds?'

He had not. He had repeated most of his other stories, but this one was new. I waited eagerly.

'Leeds was where it all started.' His words came slow and quiet. I suspected he would be unconscious soon. 'Where the tramping began. Back then, if I had the money I'd go to the pub. I don't any more. Too expensive. And the funny thing is I've now got a taste for this cheap shit. Good vodka makes me sick. But back then I drank cider, ruddy *shitloads* of it. I had been blacking out for a while, but didn't think much on it. One night, my last memory was in the pub with my mates. Next thing, I came to, and I was down this weird back-alley I didn't recognise. I was in nothing but my pants and a pint-bottle of cider in my hand. There were two women in front of me, younger than me, but not girls. One was shouting at me. Horrible things. I smashed the bottle over her head and then stuck the other one in the guts. I ran away. I haven't been back to Leeds since.'

I heard the hollow thud of an empty bottle on the concrete floor, watched as the stub of a cigarette drifted down and gently extinguished itself. I felt sick. Stan had already passed out, and I backed from his garage and out on to the street. The London story had been upsetting. This one horrified me. I did not want to see Stan again. Everything had changed:

all that drunken jollity was now stomach-churning and nightmarish.

And it was about to get worse.

||

Aimless, lost in drunken and swampy reflection, wanting nothing more than my sleeping bag and closed eyes, I pushed forward. It was gone midnight. I was so tired I could have slept in the river, but while alcohol bred fatigue it also bred obstinacy, and I was determined to make it back to the woods. By luck alone, I found my bearings at the southern edge of Greville Smyth Park. I had always avoided it after dark for it was large and unlit and intimidating, but I was drunk enough to be glad to see it. I knew that, walking through it, I could get on the right track 'home'.

A path began at the entrance and then forked off in myriad directions. I chose one which ran along the periphery of the park towards the river. Halfway along, I could dimly make out a globulous and moving mass in the darkness. As I drew closer, I saw it was nine teenagers clustered in an adventure playground twenty metres or so from the path. I heard the unmistakeable fizzing sounds of opened cans and unscrewed plastic bottle lids. A young and female voice sounded out above them.

'If yer wash yer dick, mate, I'll suck it for yer. Aww, that's right. Yer han't got nowhere to wash, have yer?'

All nine shrieked with laughter. I carried on walking. One of the boys, attempting to match the courage of his female friend, shouted: 'Oi, mate, she's fucken talken to yer!'

I continued to walk, head down.

'Fucken hobo scum!'

I did not look at them as I moved on. I was drunk enough not to feel particularly frightened – indeed, my overwhelming sensation was one of pity for the poor teachers who would have those kids in class tomorrow.

As the path rounded a corner and momentarily left the park to cut through a slim underpass, I became aware of someone following me. Shaped by the play of light from the road, a long and marching shadow stretched out before me, and I could somehow tell from the hunch, the quick steps, the hands in pockets, that it was cast by a male. Perhaps, I thought, it was one of the teenagers. Here to test his bravado. Hollering 'Fucken hobo scum!' had not been enough to impress. The thought worried me. It was one thing to shout insults at a lone, passing stranger; quite another to track him.

As the path rejoined the park and curved around another corner, I took the opportunity to cast an innocent and cursory glance behind me. The man I glimpsed was too old to be one of the teenagers. I continued to walk. Ahead was another underpass. It was dark and secluded. I changed direction. Another path led up to the road, where it was bright and loud. I walked up it.

At the top, I understood I had made the wrong decision. The short path led down again into another underpass far larger than the one I had avoided. The man was still behind me. I considered sprinting across the dual carriageway, but it was dotted with 60 mph cars, and anyway I would have to vault the five-foot-high railings to get on to it.

Stay calm, I thought.

I came to the top of the steps down. I should have stopped walking, should have stayed above, leaned over the railings and pretended to watch the traffic. The man would surely pass, but what was to stop him waiting for me below? I could turn around, but that would lead me back into the park. If this man wanted to kick me to death, as my thumping heart suggested, then he would find only an applauding audience in those caustic teenagers – perhaps one could even film the beating on their smartphone.

Anyway, I reasoned, stopping would do me no favours, would betray my building anxiety. This man only knew me from the lines of my back. He had no idea who I was or what I was capable of. The enigma was the ball in my court. If he was going to attack, he was weighing it up, judging the risks, the potential falls. I am not a big man, but neither am I small. I pushed my shoulders back and pulled my hands from my pockets, clenching them into obvious fists. I was not a fighter, but I could pretend to be one. I knew from countless travels across the globe to seemingly dangerous countries that most victims looked like victims. Avoiding it was a question of visible self-confidence.

Don't panic, I thought.

I descended the steps and entered the underpass. It seemed to be made for crime. The kind of place people come to get murdered. The darkness was blackness, neglected by the refracted headlights of the cars above. Twenty metres wide and a hundred long, interrupted by a dozen thick pillars wide enough to obscure even the heaviest man from sight, it pulsed, spun, and enveloped me in fear.

Maintain, I thought.

I had been counting the acoustics of his footsteps. Until then, they had matched my own. But in the underpass their sudden acceleration bounced off the concrete ceiling, and I knew he would be at my side in seconds.

Fuck, I thought.

He touched my elbow.

'You want summin?' he said.

'No.'

'Cos I can get you summin,' he said.

'No.'

'Look, bruv.' His hand, still on my elbow, began to pinch, and we both stopped. 'I know you got no money. I ain't *arksing* you to pay me nuffin. But I can sort you out.'

For the first time, I looked him in the eye. His face was taut and wrinkle-free, young, and his cheekbones looked sharpened. An oversized Adam's apple bobbed up and then down his sinewy throat as he swallowed, and the motion looked painful.

'What you got?' I asked.

'Evryfin.' He smiled, and the missing incisors seemed to make the rest of his teeth jut forward beyond his shrinking lips.

I should have maintained my negativism, said one final 'No' and continued walking. But his offer intrigued me. Not because I wanted any of his wares, but because he seemed to be offering a one-on-one credit system. The audacity of his enterprise was shocking, and I saw in an instant how he worked. Target the vulnerable. Get them both in debt and hooked. Keep them coming back. Make him the world. Then bleed them for everything they had or would have. Work on the addiction. Work on the temporary highs. What else does a homeless person have in their lives?

I wanted none of this, but I did want clarification.

'Are you saying you're going to give me something for nothing?' I asked.

He released my elbow and stepped back. I saw his face, eyebrows raised and lips quivering, and realised what had happened. It was my voice. Up until then, my monosyllables had masked it. But my final question had betrayed me.

'Who are you?' he said, hands back in pockets and feet turning to ten to two. 'You fuckin' police? What you doin' here?'

'No...' I faltered, '... I'm not...'

'What you doin' here?'

'I'm... no...'

'Is this a set-up? What you doin' here? *What you doin' here?*'

I ran. There was no conscious decision. I don't remember starting. One minute I was locked in paralysis, the next I was running full-pelt. It was instinctive. Response became mechanism. I ran faster than the fear-fuelled adrenalin which coursed through my veins. Neither the weight of my knapsack nor its bungeeing rhythm against my back slowed my acceleration, and I cleared the underpass and the path back up into the light in thoughtless seconds. Finally, I stopped and looked behind. He had not followed me.

CHAPTER FIVE

WESSEX WATERWAYS

I

It takes a long time to enter a city on foot, and a long time to leave it, too. The city crumbles as it peters out, and its diminuendo can seem endless. Beyond the bus station and the railway underpasses, beyond the motorway even, the no-man's-land between city and country can be a frightening place with its industrial estates, its graffitied terraces, its unfriendly locals.

My head throbbed and my body ached as I walked. The alcohol which clawed at my blood cells was the root, but the fear and disgust of the previous day's revelations left me feeling equally sick. The night had held little sleep, just three hours of catatonic unconsciousness followed by awful dreams I awoke from at patchy intervals which I could not remember but which left the physical imprints of a thudding heart and a sweat-soaked brow. I rose before five o'clock, packed my belongings and, too anxious for breakfast, walked along the side of the River Avon with the sole intention of putting Bristol as far behind me as possible.

It was only by Canham, miles from the centre, that the transformation seemed finally complete: where city became country; where concrete became gravel and mud; where young men with baseball caps, low-slung trousers and pimp-walks became motionless fishermen and dog-walkers; where council houses became trees and the occasional riverside palace; and where modified Fords and Subarus became barges, riverboats and faux paddle steamers for sightseers journeying along the river between the West Country's two great cities: Bristol and Bath.

With the topographical metamorphosis came my own translation. The morning's sickness dissipated as the trees grew and the city dissolved. Thought became coherent and rational, unlike the fleeting flashes of regret and white-hot panic which had dogged my initial footsteps. Visions of the dealer, our mutual horror at that single moment, the view of my pounding feet and the walls of a tunnel, played through my mind like a glitching DVD. But it was Stan I always came back to. He would, I knew, wake in his garage soon, find me gone, think little of it, make his slow way down to The Wild Goose. He would sit at the table we had made our own, perhaps slide the free seat closer to him in case anyone tried to take it, silently rehearse a story to tell me. I felt guilty I would not be there, would perhaps never see him again, but the guilt slid into repugnance when I remembered his final story, and that led to images I could not shake while Bristol's walls remained: glass shards in a bleeding stomach, matted hair, fingers picking and poking at a torn gut, a red pool in a litter-strewn alley.

My only answer was to walk away from it all.

2

The walk helped, too: one of the best cures for a hangover I know. I was hungry again, and suddenly parched. It was agreeable to recognise such primitive desires. The strange sight of four ponies grazing on the escarpment beneath the A4 flyover would have sent me into an hallucinatory panic an hour earlier, but by now they became merely another odd instance on this weird journey, and I settled into the slope opposite theirs to boil noodles and neck water while a thousand cars played a ceaseless and resonating minor chord overhead.

It felt good to be beside water again, to be *moving* again. Up and along this river lay Bath, and my feet seemed determined to reach it as swiftly as possible. At times, they even seemed to want to send me into a run. Perhaps I was still drunk. Stan's cheap vodka, I imagined, had a nuclear half-life.

At Hanham, the river arced north, passing the extinguished Cadbury's factory where, inspired by Roald Dahl's childhood stories, I had hoped to one day become a professional chocolate-taster; through miles upon miles of lived-in, stationary longboats alongside docks with barbecues, washing-lines and TV aerials; and then finally out into the open to wind below the undulations of the Cotswolds. These gentle hills felt like a watershed, for with them I finally left 'the West'.

Noon came, with it a lunch of beans and bread, and I left the river to join the Bristol and Bath Railway Path. I had meant to spend the night in Bath who, elegant lady that she is, gave the impression that even her rough sleepers would be of a superior quality, but Bristol had quenched my city-fix for now, and as soon as the concrete began I was eager to leave again.

I skirted the city past its ladder of locks and pushed on along the Kennet and Avon canal. Here was a protracted nose-to-tail line of longboats which jostled for position about the mooring posts whose maximum staying-time steadily increased – twenty-four hours, forty-eight, seventy-two – as they and I got further away from the city centre. Beyond that, staying-time became unlimited, and it seemed that the boats did, too. Moored permanently and lived in, their roofs were cluttered with car batteries, petrol generators, solar panels, chopped firewood and plastic sacks of charcoal; their path-side windows blacked out or boarded up; bicycles leaned against rotting gangplanks; potted, overgrown gardens on bow or stern or both; empty wine bottles and crushed beer cans on totemic display; old canoes and kayaks either tethered to the side or left upside down in the nearby hedgerow. Painted in primary-colour Hammerite, the longboats had names like *Loose Goose, Grimalkin, The Great Escape, Daisy, Celt, Tilly, Border Raider, Tanith: Tough Bros of Teddington* and *Only Dead Fish Go With The Flow*. I saw few people among them, more frequently a lazy cat perched on the roof or a happy, bouncing dog which tumbled about the towpath or barked at me from the safety of a porthole window. Those people I did see were often older and shirtless, barefooted, working on the boat or calming the yapping dog; two cycled past in suits from their day at work to leave their bikes on the grass and lower their heads to enter their boat-homes; another paddled along the canal in his kayak, stepping from his smaller boat to his larger, and carrying with him a briefcase. They were city-workers, living on water in pursuit of an alternative lifestyle away from the suburbs, or because real estate prices in those suburbs had become unfeasible; not homeless, but houseless nonetheless.

3

My own lodgings that night were found beside one of these longboats, where a miniature lay-by slipped off from the towpath and down into a cleared thicket in the woods. A heap of grey ash denoted a recent fire, and from one of the lower branches of a sycamore on the periphery hung a crude sign with pink letters stencilled on to it: *Jimbo's Jungle*. It felt like one of the many dens my brother, my dog and I had made in the woodlands around our childhood Cornish village, and when I slept there that night I dreamed of red-tipped matches and self-made fires.

I woke in the morning with a thin frost of dew across my sleeping bag. Each night was getting colder, but out here, away from the concrete, it seemed far more palatable than in the city. The sun rose and I laid my belongings out on the towpath to dry while I washed, cleaned my teeth and prepared breakfast. Three boats down, a dog barked, voices mumbled, and the barge began to lazily rock from side to side. I dipped my feet into the canal. A cold burn rose to my ankles and I pulled them out before I lost my toenails. Gasping but happy, I towelled off and shouldered my knapsack. A young woman in a dressing gown appeared from her boat with a mug of tea in hand and stared at me. I smiled, and walked on.

Not long after, I came across three young men, perhaps nineteen years old, squatting at the water's edge. One had his mobile phone laid out on the grass, and tinny dance music beat from its small speaker. Beside it lay a supermarket carrier bag, and one of the lads reached into it to share out cans of energy drinks and a packet of cigarettes. They stared at me as I drew close. The middle one took another phone from his pocket, placed it to his ear and murmured into it, his eyes never leaving me as I passed. *What are you doing here?* I thought. *It's eight in the morning!*

Some yards later, the path rounded a corner and I stopped, pretending to innocently look at the row of riverside houses which had sprung up, and glanced behind me. The three lads were on their feet, following me, cans in right hands and cigarettes in mouths, one with the carrier bag, the other still with his phone at his ear.

Adrenalin spiked as I walked on, quicker than my usual pace. *Not again*, I thought. *You're paranoid. You were bullied in Mawgan Porth and scared in Bristol, but not every young man wants to take advantage of the nearest tramp. Get a grip.*

But I *was* paranoid, and the hectoring inner monologue couldn't assuage that. On this towpath, I realised, there was no means of escape, no direction to go but forward. To my left, the back gardens of the houses were fenced off with insurmountable ten-foot railings; to my right, there was only water.

I walked faster. I did not look round again. I did not need to. My imagination had plugged into overdrive. The one with the phone, I decided, had called friends. *There's an old pikey at the canal*, he told them. *Park up a few miles down and then walk back towards town. We'll pincer-move the fucker. Might have some cash on him. Even if he doesn't, could be fun.* I stared hard at the water. Could I swim that? The far side was only, what, ten metres? Would they follow me in?

Then, suddenly, salvation. A family – mother, father, three blonde children, an ecstatic Jack Russell – appeared from beneath a bridge a hundred metres in front. I slowed. They were loud: I could hear the children laughing. I stopped. *Ingratiate yourself*, I thought. The mother called the dog to her and picked her youngest up. The father stretched his arms around the shoulders of the other two. He was big: shaven-headed, huge pectorals visible through his tight sweatshirt. The kids disappeared into his armpits. They must have seen my stalkers. The children had stopped laughing. Their guardedness gave me comfort.

I turned around to flaunt my safety, but there was no one there. The family drew level with me. The mother and children looked at the ground. The father stared into my eyes. The dog barked. They passed. It was me they had been wary of: me with my sleep-starved, bloodshot eyes, my dirty clothes, my stupid beard and my weird smile. Those lads weren't the threat on that towpath. I was.

4

'Paranoia's a killer. Trust me there,' Nigel said. 'Looking like you do, acting like you are, you'll find most people will be far more scared of you than you are of them.'

Nigel spoke from first-hand experience. We had a lot in common: we both had homes, but we both looked homeless. The latter was the reason I had approached him, sat on a wooden bench overlooking the Kennet and Avon canal not far from Bradford-on-Avon, eating an egg-mayonnaise roll from a tinfoil wrapper and drinking from a Thermos flask. He was nearing fifty; long grey hair hanging in a loose ponytail; cheeks washed with sparse but grainy stubble; an old and pink T-shirt which frayed at the seams around his neck; wafting pantaloon trousers. He looked like a tramp, but I suspected from the lack of introversion in his gaze and the lack of hurry in his eating that he, like myself, was new to the game. He had watched me carefully as I walked towards him and, when I drew close, he beamed a toothy smile and called: 'All right, boy?'

It was time for lunch and I sat on the bench next to him, pulling out my stove and heating a tin of soup. Nigel watched with unashamed admiration as I cooked, crushing his tinfoil into a ball and announcing: 'I've got to get me one of *those*.'

I asked him where he was going and where he had come from.

'Bradford-on-Avon,' he said, answering both my questions. 'I like to walk down here for lunch sometimes. I like to walk.

I was about to set off back there, but I can wait for you. We can walk together. I'm guessing that's where you're going.'

'In that direction,' I said, 'but ultimately beyond. I suppose I could stop there for the night. Where do you sleep?'

Nigel laughed. 'In my bed,' he said. 'In my house. Sorry, boy, but if you're after a room, I can't...'

'No, no,' I interrupted, 'that's not what I meant. I'm sorry, I thought you were...'

'Homeless?'

'Homeless. A tramp.'

'Well, I'm not homeless, but I suppose I am a sort of tramp.'

I cleaned and packed my utensils and we walked along the towpath to Bradford-on-Avon together. Nigel unravelled his story along the way. He had, as he liked to call it, 'a manic case of claustrophobia'. He owned a house in Bradford, bequeathed to him by his late mother along with a sizeable inheritance. Coupled with the benefits he derived from his condition, this inheritance and paid-for property meant he did not have to work.

'The problem with claustrophobia,' he explained, 'like all idiosyncrasies, is that it gets worse as you get older. I had it mildly when I was young, but I could still go to school and sixth form. I even lasted one year at university. But that was when it really hit. I had this lecture hall which was two-tiered. I always sat on the ground floor, but the ceiling above was just over head-height, and all that weight was so much to contemplate that I ended up not being able to concentrate on the lectures. All I could think of was that thick ceiling above me, and all those other students sitting on top of it. I had a terrible panic attack one day, literally ran from the hall and caught the first train home. That was the day of my undoing. I should have ridden out the anxiety and returned the next day to fight it. But I didn't. I went home, back to Bradford, and I never left again. Weight became this fixation for me, and I could just about bear it at home when my mother was in, but never anywhere else. I got reclusive and spent the next three years in the house when Mum was there and then in the back garden when she wasn't. When she passed, I couldn't even stay in the house any more.'

For the last twenty years, Nigel's life had become a relentless pursuit of the outside world. 'I've often thought about just doing it properly,' he admitted. 'Going full-tramp. It wouldn't make much of a difference. Every waking hour I spend outdoors. And, believe me, when I'm outside, all those anxieties, all that insanity, all that weight, it doesn't even register. Sometimes I'm even grateful for my disorder: there's a lot of things I get to see normal people don't.'

'So why not do it?' I asked. 'Sell the house, live outdoors full-time on the money, go full-tramp?'

'The cold,' he replied. 'It's the bloody cold. Believe me, I've thought about buying a one-way ticket to Andalucia, taking so many drugs I pass out on the flight, but even the thought of entering a travel agent's to buy my passage, or sitting in the airport, or going through passport control on the other side…' He became visibly anxious at these thoughts, and they tailed off as he removed and shouldered his backpack five or six times.

'No,' he said finally. 'I've got a system, and it works. I'm happy with it.'

Each night, Nigel would walk to his front door when he felt himself growing tired. He had garden furniture arranged outside, and he would sit in one of the plastic chairs, take a pill, count the twenty-three minutes on his wristwatch, and then, when he felt 'the droop', would open his door. Years earlier, he had rearranged his house so that his bed lay as close to the front door as possible. Flopping into it, he would pass out for the night, wake in the morning, run outside, and calmly go to get breakfast from his favourite outdoor food stall.

'That's why I look like a tramp,' he said. 'I change my clothes at the start of each new season. This lot,' he gestured down at himself, 'this is my early-autumn attire. I've got about a month left before I'll need something warmer. All my clothes are there next to my bed. It takes a lot of willpower to stay in the house long enough to grab the next set when I need them, but I manage.'

'When was the last time you saw the rest of the house?'

'About two years after Mum died. But it's all right. I've got a cleaner. She sorts it out for me.'

We walked the last mile to Bradford quietly. Nigel was affable and charming, heroic even in his compensatory systems, but I felt deeply sorry for him. His life was lived around his claustrophobia to a degree I found startling. He was in great shape for his age, for he walked everywhere and ate well (always *al fresco*, of course), but what had his strange condition denied him? He would never marry, never find work which fulfilled his core, and what would happen to him if he suffered an injury or disease? I pictured him in a hospital bed, and despaired at the thought.

'You shouldn't worry about me, boy,' he said as we parted company at Bradford. 'My life isn't so bad. I walk, that's what I do. Everywhere. You're doing it now, and you're going to see things all those people stuck indoors for half their life will never see. That's good. It's what you should do. Walk everywhere. Except on motorways. Tried it once. Police picked me up before I'd even made a mile. Worst experience of my life being in that car. Won't be doing that again.'

5

For the next few days, I walked east along the Kennet and Avon canal. The sun shone hard, but unlike the Cornish cliffs there was shade if I needed it, and I could be more frugal with my water supply. Every night was colder, but there were always plenty of quiet and sheltered spots beside the canal – after dark, no one walked the towpaths beyond the towns – and once I slept until nine in the morning, something I had not done since Portishead.

The walk was pretty: pretty in the way England can be in September, but it rarely went beyond that, and I found myself growing bored. It seemed to take forever to reach Reading. The towns I popped up in – Devizes, Hungerford, Newbury – were always the same: small, redbrick, affable, pompous; and the towpath itself maintained such a consistency of appearance that even my daydreams became bland and uninspired, and I found myself checking my watch at ever-shortening intervals.

When Reading finally appeared, I learned from a walkers' signpost on its outskirts that I had travelled 105.5 miles from Bristol, and still had another 66.5 to London. Achievement mingled with trepidation: together they gave birth to stamina, and I pushed on.

The canal led through The Oracle: a heavily built-up part of central Reading, where Las Iguanas, Café Rouge, Mission Burrito, McDonalds and the House of Fraser coffee shop bulged out like toes dipped over the canal's edge. I felt like I had wandered out from the desert. Sunburned, crack-lipped, slight limp from a pain in my knee I had forgotten about, the half-smile of the half-mad, my teeth clean but my clothes filthy, I walked timidly through the throngs of mothers and toddlers noisily queuing for an autograph from a man in a Peppa Pig outfit. I had spent so much time on the canal from Bath alone – I had barely spoken to anyone since Nigel – that this sudden influx of people provoked a strange fear in me, and I shrank from passing shoulders and bags, as if worried I might contaminate and infect. In return for my tiptoeing and sidestepping, I was paid no heed. Some moved backwards almost imperceptibly as I approached, but most did not even notice me.

Just a mile away, the Kennet and Avon canal met the Thames. It cheered me up, for this was another watershed: the home stretch, which I intended to follow all the way to Central London. At the confluence were boats, walking families, trees, a thousand swans, and no houses. I sat on a patch of grass and boiled noodles for lunch. The old women in sun hats stared at me from the passing *Mary Stuart*, followed by four young males rowing a gig while an older man in sunglasses rode a jet ski next to them and shouted: 'Almost there... let it come to you... don't go searching... sit, sit, sit... have patience.' The whole vista – along with the perfect weather: cloudless sky and a light breeze – felt so quintessentially English that I decided to complete the landscape by taking a nap under a nearby weeping willow.

6

When Laurie Lee walked east from his Gloucestershire village of Slad in 1934, his first sight of London was from Beaconsfield. For me, in 2011, the city seemed to begin miles before, perhaps even as far away as Maidenhead. From there on, urbanity rose above the Thames-side trees and spread across the fields with increasing regularity. At Windsor, the overhead planes flew lower and lower, louder and more frequent. A cluster of palatial mansions appeared to enjoy exclusive rights to the riverbank, and the white acorns directed me away and out along a roadside.

Windsor itself was bright and rammed with tourists who took photographs of the royal castle, the royal statues and the royal mailboxes. There had not been so many tourists since Cornwall, nor so much wind. The latter seemed apt here.

I walked on without stopping, determined to reach the M25, the border-crossing to London proper. I contemplated various methods of celebration: perhaps I should sing a song, do a little dance, as I passed underneath the motorway. After all, that would be it, at that precise moment I would have walked from Cornwall to London. I had settled on London Bridge as my finishing point, but that was as arbitrary as Land's End, and I hadn't even started there. The tramp was by no means over – I had come to London to live in it homeless for a while – but the walk which surrounded it almost was, and the prospect of stepping under that motorway and appearing on the other side with arms raised and voice bellowing grew more and more exhilarating the closer I got.

Sadly, when I came to the low, elegant bridge at Bell Weir Lock, the footpath had been closed off. Following a sporadic and often contradictory string of signs, I was navigated around the A30 and through industrial estates in such a disorienting succession of right angles and U-turns that I was unsure exactly when I was under the M25 or the A30 or even on which side I was, and my grand London entrance was something of an anticlimax.

So too was my first stop: Staines. Staines was used in comedy for the same reason Slough was – its pejorative double-meaning was apt. Staines exemplified how horrible London could be. Shopping trolleys and wooden pallets lay in the river, rusting or rotting; front gardens were overgrown and unkempt, strewn with moulding toys or supermarket crates; rubbish bins overflowed and stank; the air seemed filled with wasps. On the high street, opposite Poundland, was the '98 Pence Shop'. The only thing which Staines sought to surpass itself in was mediocrity.

I bought a reduced-to-clear sandwich and sat on a bench to eat. Beside me, a man ranted passionately at another, who sat meekly nodding and chuckling. I tuned in.

'People say Cockney rhyming slang is dead. But what they don't realise is that they're using it all the time. When you say "use your loaf", do you know where it comes from? It's cockney. Loaf of *bread,* so *head.* Or if they say "barnet" to mean their hair. Comes from Barnet *Fair.* There's loads of them. *Me old China.* China *plate.* A really interesting one is when people say "aris" to mean "arse". Most people think it's just because they sound similar, or that looks like how it's spelled. Actually, it's short for *Aristotle, bottle, bottle and glass, arse.* See? Funny, that one. Same as when you say someone's *bottled it.* It's got the same meaning, cos they've lost their bottle, their bottle and glass, their arse – they've shit themselves. Same thing. I love it all. Best one was one me dad used to say when it was a bright day. He'd say "the currant's in me mincers". Currant *bun* and mince *pies.* See? That's a different one, but all those others are slang, and everyone uses them now. But they come from *Cockney* slang. They come from *London.*'

I smiled when I remembered that here, in London, the favourite topic of conversation was always London itself.

7

I scurried out of Staines and back out beyond the M25 before night fell to sleep behind the cement wall of a hotel's car park. There, I spent most of the night trying to ignore what I would do the next night – over all this time living rough, I had still not slept on *streets*, but once I was firmly ensconced in London I would have no choice. There were no cliffs nor beaches, no farmer's fields, no woodlands nor safe towpath hedgerows in the capital.

Entering London, by whatever means, always produces a feeling, be it one of excitement or trepidation or fear or nostalgia or disillusionment. One senses that the rules change when you hit London, as does the smell.

One of the walker's joys of inner-M25 London is pavements, *flat* pavements. I could have followed the Thames path to my goal, but I was tired of nature's meandering trajectories. I wanted the Roman route: straight and direct, functional, mechanically unerring. London Road was flanked by a constant pavement, and I followed it to Kew, where I stopped in a greasy spoon for ham, egg and chips, a capital breakfast.

Over my meal, the creeping anticipation of the night ahead, my first night on the streets, began to loom and, once the last swig of tea joined the last chip on its plummet towards my stomach, it was all I could think of. All along London Road the temperature had steadily lowered, the sky grown relentlessly greyer and, as I returned to the Thames path at Kew, I realised the river had, too. It rained for the rest of the morning. I followed the long sheets of drizzle as they pushed east along the river.

If London started at Maidenhead, Central London started at Putney Bridge: red buses; mosaic underpasses; constant construction; hurried pedestrians and a congregation of cars; futuristic high-rises; Georgian terraces and bicycle racks; smokers under umbrellas; the inevitable, indefatigable tourists.

I began to notice less and less. Visions of a night rough in London clouded my eye-line.

At Chelsea, a line of houseboats – giants to their canal cousins – rested on the mudflats side by side. A common sign recurred amongst them: 'WE ARE A COMMUNITY. WE ARE NOT A COMMODITY.'

Where am I going to sleep tonight?

Beyond the houseboats: Albert Bridge, lathered in ship-shaped scaffolding.

Where?

Further still, on the north bank, across the river, Battersea Park, just another statue of Albert or Victoria, perhaps? I drew closer. It was not a statue, but a pagoda, within it the Buddha icon, as incongruous in London as I was.

I should go home.

A stern plaque on the last building before Vauxhall Bridge, presiding over a littered and dirty terrace: 'PRIVATE PROPERTY. IF ANYONE IS FOUND SLEEPING ON THESE PREMISES THE POLICE WILL HAVE YOU REMOVED FOR TRESPASSING.' The jarring conflict between third and second person.

This isn't fun any more. When was homelessness supposed to be fun?

The first of the skyline-icons: the London Eye, the Houses of Parliament, Big Ben.

This is it now. You're here. There's no turning back. You have to sleep here. On the streets. Unless...

An old man in his Sunday best walked along the low-tide beach, throwing stones at the wading seagulls.

Unless...

Unless I *didn't* sleep on the streets tonight. Just tonight. I had friends in Hackney happy enough and gregarious enough to offer me their couch, even if I turned up in the middle of the night with no prior warning. They were good like that, and they knew me well enough to not expect it as such, but to tolerate it when it happened. I would just spend one night, I reasoned, just enough to sleep well, wash once, and then be out again in the morning. London, for all I knew of it, and I knew it well, was too large and too anonymous to plunge straight into. I needed some time; time to gauge and assess. Though I had tramped now for well over a month, London was a different arena, and I had to prepare for it.

My resolution made, I tramped on, light again. *Just one night*, I told myself, already acknowledging it would doubtless be longer than that before I felt brave enough to join London's homeless community.

8

There were just 5 miles to go between me and London Bridge. I knew the distance because I consulted the Transport for London leaflet about the Thames path which I had picked up in the Kew cafe. Next to the map of the river I read: 'The vein of London life pumping liquid history through the heart of the Capital'. That sentence, coupled with the thought of a warm couch for the night, made me so happy that I underlined it twice and jotted down an exclamation mark at each end of the blue-drawn river. Five miles to go. Despite sore feet, my step quickened.

London, and especially this part of it, might be the most written-about city in the world. In response, I left my journal untouched in my knapsack and marched onwards.

I did, however, make one short note during those 5 miles. On the shelves of the South Bank's Foyles bookshop, where I stopped for a five-minute respite of browsing, I found a copy of my first book. I almost wept, for it had been a long time since I had seen it physically, tangibly, corporeally in a shop. Paul Theroux often wrote of discovering one of his travel books in a window display or nestled between the hands of a fellow train passenger. Sometimes, when this happened, he would reveal himself as the famous author. I considered a similar course of action in Foyles, chuckled at the thought of the blank, perhaps pitying, stares I would receive, and moved on.

With London Bridge came a surge of elation, and then a surge of exhaustion. I had no further to walk. Collapsing on the floor against the perspex sheet of a bus stop, I remembered why I had nominated this as my finishing post. A friend of mine had once cycled from Sydney to London, and he too had finished here. It took him two years, and he travelled over ten thousand miles. I had come 300 miles in less than two months, and the insignificance of my tiny tramp caused me to laugh aloud so hard it astonished me, but not the commuters around me. Perhaps if I had been dressed like them, they would have moved away. As it was, and as I looked, they remained indifferent. This made me laugh louder.

Nevertheless, there was fortuity here, for, once I calmed myself and rose to my feet, I remembered that I could hop a bendy-bus to my friends' house in Hackney for free from this very stop. Three years ago, I had done it all the time.

After half an hour, no bendy-buses had arrived or passed. This was unusual. I recalled they came every twenty minutes or so. I asked a fellow at the bus stop.

'The bendy-buses?' he snorted. 'Don't have 'em any more. Boris got rid of 'em. Brought the double-deckers back. Too many people taking the piss, riding the bendy-buses without paying.'

Rain began to fall so hard it gave me flashbacks of the night outside Hatherleigh. For the second time on the journey, I broke my rules and paid for a bus ticket to Hackney.

CHAPTER SIX

LONDON HOUSE

I

Central heating. Walls. Books on the shelves and a sitcom on the television. A pasta dinner with meat and fresh vegetables, not a baked bean in sight. Conversation. Companionship.

Staying in this house was not cheating: I was not paying for the accommodation, and my friends would not have accepted my money even if I had offered it. I was to sleep on the couch, something that surely all tramps did when they could. It was, I reasoned, acceptable – even the Compass Centre in Bristol had seemed to allow this state of being as one of the permutations of homelessness. But I could not shake the feeling – as the aftertaste of beef and red wine mingled in my throat; as Marcus told me he was getting married; as the reminiscences of student-days mayhem echoed about the room in concert with our ringing laughter – that I was emotionally and tangibly at home.

'They burned a bus right there,' Marcus said, pointing out the living-room window to the Dalston street. The infamous riots which had spread across the country less than two months before were not born here, but Hackney looters were some of the first to jump on the fiery bandwagon.

'The day before I started my walk,' I said, 'I saw Kingsland Road mentioned in a paper.' Kingsland Road was only a few steps away.

'The Turks all lined up outside their shops with baseball bats,' Dave said. 'No one fucked with them.'

'On the second night we sat right here and watched them from the window, piling up rubbish and setting it alight.'

'I was actually pretty impressed with the police. They got a lot of flak for it, but I reckon they handled things well.'

'The best bit, I was watching these three kids standing on the sidelines, getting keyed up, about to join in. Then their big sister comes out. "What the fuck are you playing at? Get in, yer stupid bastards!" She cuffs them round the head and drags them off.'

'The thing about the police is that they were *containing*. Just standing there with shields keeping all the rioters in one place. They could have got in there, made a few arrests, but then the crowd would have broken up, dispersed and caused havoc all over. Then the police would have had to chase them individually, and that's when the really bad stuff happens, down an alleyway on their own with four rioters and no support.'

'It was good to see, the next morning, all those people taking to the streets with bin bags and gloves. Community clean-up operation.'

'The media didn't portray the police right. It wasn't fair.'

It had been the same all across the country: the police had been blamed universally. With Swiftian logic, David Cameron had utilised the poor press to justify the government's decision to continue with its cuts to the police force. It was all faintly ludicrous, like responding to a flu epidemic by shutting down hospitals.

In the short moments before I fell into a deep coma on my friends' couch that first night, I decided to visit Tottenham – the trigger for the UK riots – the next day. It seemed fitting. The riots had raged as I had begun my journey. Now I was at its finishing post, a visit to Tottenham seemed a logical denouement.

I also decided I would stay a few more nights.

2

Tottenham in the morning had the air of the developing world: the slapdash markets; the shuttered bars; the charred buildings like colonial ruins; the door-to-door independent stores; fresh fruit for sale on the street; boarded-up windows; demolition sites where one expected construction sites (this was London, after all); cracked windows held in place with cling film; flat roofs; the shady money-transfer bureaus.

One burned-out building, perhaps the famous one from the papers, was in the process of demolition. Inside the walled-off enclosure, the arm of a digger swung up and into view. A single wall still stood high: brickwork, blackened plaster. Its interior side was visible, along with an extant row of books lined along an intact shelf. The digger's arm swung, breaking the wall below sight, and the books tumbled into the pit.

Upon the enclosure's exterior, permanent-marker graffiti splashed across the whitewashed plywood:

Bringing unity back into the community
Put down the guns & knives and lets live nice!
Spurs win the League Tottenham will be a better place X

I did not know why I was there. My journey was not about riots, it was about the streets – granted, some of them streets upon which riots had taken place, but these Tottenham streets had long been abandoned. Packs of commuters huddled at bus stops, passed only by long lines of sealed cars. Even London's hardy cyclists seemed absent here. Men sat and glowered over their quiet market stalls, and when I entered the main road's shops the cashiers looked me up and down with evident surprise. I thought perhaps street life would be intensified in Tottenham, but I was wrong. If anything, it had been frightened, and the streets here were as quiet as Hatherleigh.

I walked back down Stoke Newington Road, aiming for Central London. I had an Oyster Card in my pocket: Marcus had lent it to me (he was always full of generosity, it helped him reconcile being a banker in the City), but my feet seemed to need the mileage, and I gladly gave it to them. Passing a shop with the proud sticker 'This is a PORN FREE newsagent' plastered across its window, I reflected on the dearth of homeless people I had seen since crossing the M25 ley-line.

Perhaps the single passage of Orwell which has remained in my memory more than any other – even over Room 101 rats and the animal revolution – comes from his own least favourite book, *A Clergyman's Daughter*. The protagonist, Dorothy, suffering from amnesia, is reduced to homelessness on the streets of Central London. Wandering along Waterloo Road late one night, she arrives at Trafalgar Square. Here she spends the next nine days and ten nights of her itinerant life, joining the group of homeless who congregate there after dark each night. The dozen or so individuals who form the group come from all walks of life, testament to Orwell's unerring notion that anyone, no matter from whence they came, under the right set of circumstances can find themselves homeless. Amongst the brigade are Deafie, who likes to sing; Mrs Bendigo, whose husband earns four pounds a week busking in Covent Garden while she has to do a 'starry' upon Trafalgar's flagstones; the educated and verbose Mr Tallboys, a defrocked priest; The Kike, whose favourite exclamation is 'Oh Je-e-e-*eeze*!'; the indefatigable and inquisitive Charlie (always my favourite), who sings for money outside London pub doorways at Christmas; Florry, the crab-ridden prostitute; Daddy, the old-timer who has been on the road for fifty years; and of course Dorothy in the middle of them all, so cold and disoriented that she can barely remember if she has feet.

This merry and spirited band, bitter at their collective misfortune but still alive and clucking nonetheless, people the centrepiece-chapter of Orwell's novel. As I re-entered the realm of the Congestion Charge, Capital Central, I turned west and made my way towards Trafalgar Square, confident that I might find my own band and slip into their envelope as easily as Dorothy had with hers. I felt fortunate for the time on my hands. With the Dalston couch available to return to when I needed it, I could seek out companions and then join them, rather than slipping behind the first green bin I found and uneasily closing my eyes. It was another privilege I knew most tramps were not afforded, that to do this right I should march to Embankment or Blackfriars Bridge, wait until nightfall, and slap my sleeping bag down on the nearest patch of concrete.

But London's streets frightened me, and I felt the need to bide my time. As I learned later, such fear was justified.

3

I walked two laps around Trafalgar Square, checking each of the thousand or so pedestrians for any sign of vagrancy. There was none. I scanned the nooks about the National Gallery, the tiers at the base of Nelson's Column and the benches around the edge, sitting down on one myself for the next hour and timing it by the Olympic Countdown Clock, but all the people I passed and all the people who passed me were clearly not homeless. Perhaps I was here at the wrong time of day. Men in black and red jackets with officer's caps and epaulettes which read 'Heritage Warden' patrolled the square, changing direction randomly and at right angles like bluebottles. I wondered what time they finished work. I should have to return after that. Clearly, no homeless stayed here while they were on duty.

I remembered someone. When I had last spent time in London, I had on occasion frequented a pub on Leicester Square. There, in the subterranean toilets next to the tiny park, an old tramp was always present, no matter what time or day. I walked towards it, finding when I arrived that almost all of Leicester Square had been cordoned off for construction work. The toilets were closed and inaccessible. What was going on in London, not just the Capital of England, but the Capital of the Homeless? Had some clandestine clean-up operation under that shock-blonde mayor 'disappeared' them all over the last few years? Had the scourge of the streets been wiped clean for the Olympics?

I sat on the ballast holding down a temporary fence around Leicester Square's park, and I contemplated. Perhaps I should walk to Manchester. There were always homeless there. My feet squealed a resounding 'yes!'. Keep walking.

Maybe I will, I thought. But, first, I wanted to spend some more time with my friends.

4

The boys took me to a Dalston pub that night, and I grew drunk on three pints. Largely teetotal since the start of my journey, excluding my time with Stan, the sudden surge of beer and conviviality left me reeling. Bryn arrived and I enveloped him in a pissed embrace, though I had only met him a few times before.

'Where were you last night?' I hollered in his ear. He also lived in the Dalston house, but I had not seen him the evening of my arrival.

Bryn smiled shyly, took a long draught from the pint Marcus had ready for him, and sat down. 'Last night? You scared the shit out of me last night! It's late, it's dark, there's a knock at the door, Marcus goes to answer it, I stand at the top of the stairs, and all I can see is this bloody *tramp* in the doorway! I know now that you asked Marcus if he had a spare couch for the night, but that's not what I heard.'

Bryn's girlfriend, Jo, laughed into her drink. 'Tell Charlie what you thought he said.'

'I swear I heard you say "You got any spare *cash*?". And then Marcus goes "Yeah, sure" and bloody lets you in! I thought, what's going on? Some tramp going door to door in the middle of the night asking for change *and we've just invited him in*! I'll be honest. I ran into the bathroom. And I locked the door.'

Tim, another of the housemates, arrived an hour later. I accompanied him to the bar for the next pint and explained my journey thus far.

'I did something similar when I finished my A levels,' he said. 'Caught a bus down from Cumbria to London and spent a week living in Cardboard City taking photographs. You ever heard of it?'

I had. Cardboard City was one of the largest concentrations of homeless people London had seen since World War Two. In 1983, a makeshift shanty town slowly emerged and then exponentially built up along the underpasses of the Bullring roundabout near Waterloo Station. For the next fifteen years, the flimsy walls of Cardboard City grew to house, at its peak, around two hundred rough sleepers. Portrayed by the media as a tangible indictment of the Thatcher years, the thriving ecosystem may not have been caused by the Tory government, but certainly correlated with it.

'Yeah, well, it's all gone now,' Tim said. 'Burned down not long after I left. Some fuckers poured petrol over the whole place one night and set a match to it.'

This was untrue. In 1998, Lambeth Council finally won the eviction order it had sought for so long. At that time, only thirty rough sleepers remained in Cardboard City. All of them were offered free housing by the council, though it remains to this day unclear how many took it.

'I've heard there's a new one, though,' Tim continued. 'Under Hammersmith Flyover. You should check it out. If it's anything like the old one, it'll be an eye-opener.'

It was close to midnight when we walked back through Dalston's streets towards the house. I scanned the pavements and alleyway-tributaries for rough sleepers, but there were none, only the legions of hipsters with their imaginative footwear and ludicrous hairstyles. There seemed no space on these Hackney streets for the homeless, filled as they were with young and fashionable night-walkers who took it upon themselves to piss against the walls and vomit into the wheelie-bins.

5

I slept later than usual and rose feeling lethargic, unsure whether to remain in London or tramp north. Opting for indecision and, with it, the morning off, I went to visit the British Library, only to discover once I arrived that to gain access to the book rooms one had to register, and that to register one had to produce proof of address. I had none. *Another reason I could never be truly homeless*, I thought. *No library cards*.

With no other idea what to do or where to spend the rest of my morning, I returned to Trafalgar Square. Summer was by now far behind, but the autumn still fought the Baltic onslaught of winter, and the morning had grown warm and pleasant. I fancied I might sit on a bench in the square and summarise my future plans – more likely, I would read for an hour or two, or perhaps people-watch. I was, I realised, putting things off. But that did not matter so much. In all likelihood, most tramps had the same mentality.

On my way to Trafalgar Square, I pictured it as I knew it: the perpetual flow and surge of holidaymakers and school-groups, locked in their tight but merry bands, rubbing shoulders with others but never making eye contact, except when an amorous teenager found the gaze of another beyond the fountain, or an ignorant stroller passed the lens of a poised camera and Latinate invectives bounced without acknowledgement off the back of his head – all this gave the loner, me, a womb of anonymity which I could gratefully and quietly float inside.

I liked London for this. Travelling alone, which I almost always do, I find I become the immediate oddity not because of the language I speak or the colour of my skin or the style of my dress or the quirks of my expressions (all of which, in many of the places I have travelled, are alien), but because I am the loner in a gregarious world. But if London is defined by any culture, it is the culture of indifference. Watch London street performers. See how hard they try. They have to, it is the only way they can raise even the eyebrow of a passer-by in this city of eight million passers-by. In London, self is key; in London, solipsism is the universal philosophy.

This was why I liked London: every spiral of the human condition was on display there, and you could watch and listen to them all without fear of reciprocal scrutiny. I was just another tramp, another wasted existence, and who would notice me on a Trafalgar Square bench? Homeless flock to Central London because the streets are clean and the tourists have money to chuck, but they also come because, in London, everyone is ignored.

However, when I reached Trafalgar Square, I found it transformed. Sitting on a bench was out of the question. The entire square had been converted into a multimedia extravaganza to celebrate 2012's Paralympic Games. A racetrack, a tennis court and a miniature football pitch had been laid across the flagstones; tourists with upheld smartphones jostled for position with television crews and a giant screen presided over it all, showing footage of the Mayor of London, Boris Johnson, conversing earnestly with the Chair of the London Organising Committee for the Olympic Games, Sebastian Coe. Something jarred as I looked at the screen, a kind of *jamais vu*, as I realised that the little hooded tramp's head peering out above a small crowd of Chinese tourists in the corner of the screen was mine. I turned around. The mayor was just a few yards away. How wonderful it would be, I thought, to get a quote from him.

Standing amongst the crowd, I vacillated nervously and debated how feasible it would be to approach him, what I might say or ask. A hand cupped my elbow. I turned to face its owner and found the eyes of a helmeted police officer.

'Hello, mate,' he said, ushering me away from the crowd and to a corner where two free-standing billboards met. His colleague flanked my other side. 'Mind stepping over here a minute for a quick chat?'

'Love to,' I grinned. 'I enjoy a good conversation. Don't get the chance for many these days.'

'No offence or anything, mate,' he said, pulling a notebook from his pocket, 'but I saw you here with your hood up and your bag, and just wanted to ask a few questions.'

'No problem at all,' I replied, taking my journal from my pocket. 'I'd like to ask you some questions, too, if that's all right.'

'Course you can, mate. In fact, give me that book and I'll write down my details.' He scrawled his full name and officer number on to the paper. I looked up at his colleague, and she smiled warmly at me. 'Now, how about your details?'

I gave him my real name and address – I saw no reason not to, he was polite and I liked him – and he jotted them down.

'Just arrived in London?'

'Pretty much.'

'What's in the bag? Anything I should know about?'

'Here,' I said, dropping it from my shoulders and holding it out to him. 'Have a look yourself, if you like.'

'No, no, I don't need to do that. Nothing in there that could blow up, is there?'

'I've got an aerosol can.'

'Ah, mate.' He shook his head wisely. 'You can't tag around here.'

'It's deodorant.'

His colleague laughed.

'Any illegal or subversive...' he paused, '... *literature*?'

'Depends on your opinion of Dickens.'

'Never read him.'

'You should.'

'So what you up to in London? What's the plan?'

'Just walking.'

'What, you walked here from Cornwall, did you?' he laughed.

'Precisely.'

He seemed taken aback by that, and I saw the opportunity to ask some of my own questions.

'Hypothetically,' I said, 'if I were to tell you I had just arrived in London with no money and nowhere to stay, what advice would you give me?'

He looked at me. 'You need a place for the night?' There was genuine concern in his eyes and voice.

'Actually, no. I'm staying with some friends in Dalston. I'm not homeless. I walked here from Cornwall because I'm writing a book about tramping, and part of what I'm trying to discover is what it's like to be homeless in today's world. So. Say if I was homeless. What would you tell me?'

'Officially, I'm supposed to tell you to go to the youth hostel, but that's twenty quid a night and most homeless can't afford it. Or I should direct you to one of the refuges, but you'd be *very* lucky to get in there. If you'd already tried all those, I'd say go to Charing Cross Police Station. There's a soup kitchen there and a Homeless Team who might be able to help you.'

'And unofficially?'

'Unofficially…' He thought for a moment. 'Unofficially, I'd say go down to Fleet Street and The Strand. A lot of people sleep there after dark. It's fairly safe.'

'And if I went down there and spent the night, I wouldn't get arrested or moved on?'

He shook his head. 'Technically, you wouldn't be breaking any laws. Those are public by-ways. Everyone has the legal right to sleep there if they want. We would only move you on if you were in, say, a shop doorway, because then you'd be on private property. Or if you were causing an obstruction. But we're not monsters, you know? Homelessness is rife in London, and my heart goes out to those poor buggers. If we moved them on, they'd only end up somewhere else. It's hassle for them and it's hassle for us.'

We shook hands as I shouldered my bag, ready to join the crowd again. He had not once attempted intimidation or invasion during our conversation, and I was grateful for his candour.

'You know what you should do?' he said as I was about to leave. 'Try asking those two some questions. There's a few I'd like to ask them myself.' He pointed down to the makeshift tennis court. Four men in wheelchairs had been playing a doubles game when I last looked. Now, two had left and, joining the remaining two, one for each team, were Boris Johnson and the Prime Minister, David Cameron.

'You read my mind,' I said.

'Doubt you'll get to Cameron, but I hear Boris is very approachable. And if you can't get to him here, just follow him. He walks everywhere.'

I laughed at this policeman's advice – *if you can't get to him here, just follow him* – and moved off towards the tennis court.

True enough, following the game Cameron was at all times surrounded by an impenetrable pack, and as he left the court and walked towards his waiting car, I could not reach him. I returned to the tennis court, where the mayor gave interviews to a score of cameras. A woman in her seventies leaned over the railings at the sidelines, and each time the mayor looked ready to move on, she called out in an increasingly demanding sing-song: 'Boris! *Boris*!' If any member of the public was going to get his attention, it would be her. I quietly moved into position beside her.

The mayor's interviews finished. My neighbour began to swing her arms over the railings and holler his name in rapid couplets. He walked towards us. Before he could stop, she grasped his arm and pulled him towards the railings with an astonishingly powerful jerk.

'Now, Boris,' she said maternally. 'When you come up for re-election, what do you intend to do for us pensioners?'

He placed a hand over hers and gently moved it down from his forearm to his fingers, where he cupped it between both his palms and said: 'I will demand that you get the twenty-four-hour Freedom Pass that you deserve.'

'Good,' she replied with satisfaction, removing her hand from his and placing it in her pocket. 'Good.'

He made to move away and I lurched forward.

'Mr Johnson!' I called. He stopped and faced me. 'May I ask you a very quick question?'

'Of course,' he mumbled.

'If I had just arrived in London with no money and no place to stay, what advice would you give me?'

Before he could respond, a male voice from behind me called out: 'At least give him a tenner, Boris!' A peal of laughter followed, and I turned around to see sixty people clustered behind me. They fell silent and focused their attention on me and the mayor. I looked back at him. He had laughed along with the rest, but now looked nervous.

'It's all right,' I said. 'I don't want a handout. I just want information.'

My words seemed to cause him relief. 'I would tell you,' he said, 'to go to St Mungo's.' He spelled it for me, including the apostrophe. 'Or look into an organisation I work very closely with called "No Second Night Out".'

It was a politician's stock response, but I appreciated it. Dare I say it, I found myself a little star-struck, and the notes I quickly made while he spoke to me betrayed a shaking hand. I thanked him and pushed my way out of the crowd. A hand patted me on the shoulder. 'Good luck to you, mate,' a voice said. A few moments later, I realised that I was grinning.

Walking down into St James's Park, I found a quiet patch and sat down to boil noodles and note down my Trafalgar Square conversations. Rough sleepers, more than I had seen anywhere else in London so far, lay at sporadic intervals across the grass: coats for pillows; shoes and socks beside their heads. Squirrels and pigeons scurried about their bare feet. *So this is where they come during the day*, I thought. *Good choice*. The ground was soft and comfortable, the air dry and warm, and if I had been tired I could have happily stretched out there and slept myself.

But I was energised by the notes I made, and soon set off again back towards the concrete. Along Pall Mall, the day's second unanticipated opportunity walked past me. It was Jeremy Paxman, and he was alone. I stopped and watched him as he walked away. Perhaps the Mayor of London did not have a vested interest in London's homeless, but he doubtless had opinions. But Jeremy Paxman? I knew him from the television and the few books of his I had read, and not once had I heard him pass comment on homelessness.

Fuck it, I thought, *why not?*

I ran after him.

He came to a stop upon the Crimea Monument traffic island. With no pedestrian crossings and a sudden surge of traffic impeding his passage, it had trapped him perfectly. I darted between cars and sidled up next to him.

'Excuse me, Mr Paxman,' I said meekly. 'May I ask you a very quick question?'

'Yes?' He raised his eyebrows, and I felt suddenly terrified. His television persona resounded in my mind, and I feared the damning retort he would offer my impudent inquiry.

'What's your opinion of the state of homelessness in London at the moment?'

Jeremy Paxman folded his arms and leaned back against the pillar beneath the statue of Florence Nightingale. After a moment's contemplation, he said, 'I find it very troubling.'

I quickly noted down his comment, aware that he was taking in my attire.

'Are you homeless?' he asked.

'No,' I admitted. 'I'm a writer. I'm researching a book about homelessness.'

He raised his eyebrows again. 'Well, good for you!' he said. 'I'm involved with a few centres not far from here. You must visit them and spend some time there. One's called Anchor House. It's in the East End.'

'I'll tell them you sent me,' I said.

'Do. And you should visit a few other places while you're at it. The Passage at Victoria. Or St Mungo's. There's another in the centre, though they're a Roman Catholic organisation...' His sentence trailed off, and I was unsure why. I hazarded a guess that he perhaps disagreed with the religious aspect.

'Do you think they help the homeless for indoctrination rather than altruistic purposes?' I asked.

He laughed and pointed a large hand at my chest. 'That's a very cynical question, and you should be ashamed of it.'

I blushed with pride. Jeremy Paxman had just called *me* cynical.

'No, they're not like that,' he continued. 'They're a good organisation doing good things. You're not doing an Orwell, are you?'

'Kind of,' I admitted. 'I wanted to see what it was like to be a tramp in the twenty-first century, and find out why there are so few around these days.'

'Oh, tramps disappeared a long time ago.'

'Not that long,' I remonstrated. 'I remember them from when I was a kid, and I'm not that old.'

'True. I'm a lot older than you, and I remember them well. Don't know why there aren't any any more. Is it because we're so affluent now? Or because we're so atomised and suspicious of everyone else, especially people on the streets? That's the main problem in general, I think, why homelessness still exists. People don't want to help the homeless because they are fundamentally frightened of them.'

'That's what I think. It's fear from ignorance. Most people don't know anyone who is or has been homeless, and they don't understand why or how it can happen. They're ignorant, and that makes them frightened, and that makes them contemptuous.'

'I've been guilty of it myself. I remember a conversation I had with a man in Manchester. He had been a printer, but then his job became obsolete with the digital revolution, and he ended up on the streets. I remember realising then that the homeless are just ordinary people, too, and that it can happen to anyone given the wrong set of circumstances.'

'Have you read *Stuart* by Alexander Masters?' I asked.

'Yes, I know the one. The biography about the homeless man in Cambridge.'

I nodded. 'At one point, Stuart says that the first time he met middle-class people he was shocked to discover how ordinary they were.'

He laughed, then stopped and looked about him, perhaps suddenly cognisant of the fact that he had just spent the last few minutes talking to a stranger who dressed and smelled like a tramp. 'Anyway!' he announced. 'Good luck with your work.'

I thanked him profusely for his time and generosity, and turned to go back the way I had come. Five steps on, I heard him shout behind me. He was stood at the lip of the pavement.

'You *have* read Orwell's *Down and Out*, haven't you?' he asked.

'Of course. Orwell's my hero.'

'Good,' he said, and crossed the road.

6

I returned to the Dalston house to pass a few hours online researching Boris Johnson's hint at the 'No Second Night Out' campaign.

Launched in April 2011, the No Second Night Out (NSNO) initiative began in London (its tag line was 'Ending Rough Sleeping in London by the end of 2012'), but has since been taken up by local authorities across the country. Looking at the important fact that, of the approximately four thousand rough sleepers in London, well over half (about two thousand, three hundred) are new to the streets, it aims to target those new homeless and ensure that they are rehoused within their first twenty-four hours of rough sleeping.

It is a bold objective, but one which, by and large, has met with considerable applause by many who already worked to reduce homelessness. Networking and offering extra funding to outreach programmes, homeless shelters and refuges, soup runs, voluntary and council-led services, NSNO has, at the time of writing, already helped a thousand rough sleepers to reconnect with their families in London, elsewhere in the UK or even abroad, and has nudged a subject which has been taboo for far too long into the public consciousness. One of the scheme's most successful implementations is a hotline telephone number which members of the public can call if they see someone sleeping rough. NSNO pledges to send out assistance to anyone whose location and details are phoned in.

Like most state-led schemes which aim to help the disadvantaged, No Second Night Out has met with some criticism. Most is inconsequential, but some is worth noting here. One revolves around the strange parameters NSNO works by – that is, that only people literally *sleeping on the streets* can be helped by the scheme. If a hotline phone call reveals a person sleeping in a stairwell or car park, they are deemed outside of the jurisdiction of NSNO's remit, and no one will be sent to offer them assistance.

One recent news story reported the experience of a voluntary worker who met a rough sleeper in an Islington McDonald's. Sitting next to him, she succeeded in engaging him in conversation, and learned that he had arrived two days before from Birmingham and was homeless. He had spent the last of his money the first night in a youth hostel, had walked the streets the second night to keep warm, and now was stuck in the city with no money, sweatshirt or sleeping bag. Someone had offered him a five-pound note on the streets that afternoon, and he was using it slowly in McDonald's so that he might keep warm for as long as possible.

Remembering No Second Night Out, the voluntary worker called the hotline and described the man she had met, only to be told that they could do nothing because they 'don't meet people in buildings'. Their advice was for him to leave the McDonald's, find a place to sleep, bed down, and then call from there. Only then might they be able to send someone out. The voluntary worker related this to the man, he reminded her about his lack of sleeping bag and sweatshirt, his lack of a *phone*, the dreadful cold outside and the warmth in the McDonald's, and then he burst into a strange laughter.

There are others who are even more cynical of the scheme. After I returned home from my journey and began my additional research for this book, I had a telephone conversation with a London-based outreach worker who, requesting anonymity, said: 'Mostly, No Second Night Out does good work and helps people. But it's the motives behind it I question. Everyone involved is constantly reminded that it is just a *pilot* project. We all know what that means. It's the Olympics. Boris wants as many people as possible off the streets for the Olympics. After that, you watch, they'll shut it down. We need something much more long-term.'

At the time of writing, months after the Olympics closing ceremony, No Second Night Out continues, and the deputy mayor has recently pledged to push the target of ending rough sleeping in London beyond the scheme's original deadline (the end of 2012). While NSNO did not meet its initial target, this is not a failure. Any project which aims to solve the issue of homelessness requires longevity and commitment, and it is my hope that, whatever the new target may be, NSNO will continue beyond that, too.

7

The front page of the *Metro* newspaper the following day seemed so cosmically apt for me that I tore it off and folded it into my journal. Two pictures of yesterday's tennis match predominated: Cameron, neck-flab bulging over his collar, eyes shut, head thrown back and thin lips sucking in air like he had just been punched in the groin; Johnson wielding his racket like an axe, hair inexplicable and jaw thrust out in a grunt of exertion. Above them both, the seemingly disconnected headline: 'Crisis on the streets.' To the right, the first seven paragraphs of an article stating that Britain's homeless population had increased by 17 per cent since the previous year and was likely to get worse.

In the hope of finding out more, I walked to Charing Cross where Westminster's Homeless Unit worked from the police station. I had no appointment and was asked to bide my time in the waiting room while they found someone who could see me. I did not lie. I was, I told the receptionist, researching homelessness in the UK and wanted their professional perspective.

An officer came out to meet me and beckoned me into a small office. I was not offered a seat.

'You're writing a book? I'm not sure I can help you. Really, you should be going through the official channels.'

'I appreciate that,' I said, 'but this book is supposed to look at the unofficial side of homelessness, the real-life side. I'm sure you could point me towards your latest online press statement with all the up-to-date statistics, but what I want is *your* perspective, as a man whose job it is to try and reduce homelessness in London.'

He squirmed uncomfortably. The door behind him was still open, and he was slowly edging towards it. 'Like I said, I can't really help you out. I don't talk to journalists.'

'I'm not a journalist.'

'No, but for me the same rules apply. How do I know you won't misquote me? Land me in trouble?'

I could read between the lines. He feared that, were he to talk candidly, he might say something his superiors would not condone. After years of teaching, I could empathise with his reluctance to speak openly about his profession. It would be too easy for it to lead to litigation or dismissal.

But I needed something more than this stonewalling. 'How about I just ask you a few things?' I said. 'Just about the process of your job. Just what you do, not why you do it. As soon as you've had enough, just say so and I'll go.'

He left the room for a few seconds and then returned. Moments later, a colleague walked in and sat to busy himself with some paperwork. I recognised that, too. The need to have someone else present. It was a small shield against the litigious potential of a one-on-one discussion. If I ever gave a detention to a single child at school, I would always make sure the door was open and another teacher was in earshot. Who knew what that child might claim later? In this situation, who knew what *I* might claim later?

'Go on, then,' he mumbled.

'What would you say is the main focus of the Homeless Unit?'

'Our main focus is to reduce the amount of rough sleepers in Westminster.'

'Just Westminster?'

'That's our area. All London would be too big for us to cover. We couldn't, for example, cope with all the homeless in Angel, as well.'

'So do they have their own Homeless Unit?'

'I don't know. I don't think so. The reason we have one here is because Westminster has the highest density of rough sleepers in London. It's constantly changing, but right now the average number we cite is eighty a night.'

That sounded to me remarkably low, and my interlocutor agreed that it was. He explained that it was not an actual figure of the homeless in Westminster – moreover, it came from literal headcounts of the people that could be found sleeping rough in one night. It did not include those who had secured a place in a hostel or refuge for the night; did not include those who had wandered off for a change of scenery after getting into trouble; did not include those who the police simply could not find.

'Remember,' he continued, 'our focus is getting the *rough sleepers* off the street. And not all homeless are rough sleepers.'

I told him about the research I had conducted into the No Second Night Out scheme which, by my reckoning, seemed to work by the same rules.

'No Second Night Out is good, I'll give you that, but we've been doing the same thing for years.'

I asked him to explain the generic strategy of the Homeless Unit when they found someone sleeping rough.

'The first step is to ascertain where you're from and see if we can reconnect you with that place. A lot of people have had an argument with their parents or partners and thought – right, I'm going to London. You'll be amazed how many people believe that cliché that the streets are paved with gold. But they're not paved with gold. The streets can be lonely and they can be very frightening. Where are you from?'

'Cornwall.'

'Right, I'd try and find out from you why you left Cornwall and if there's anyone there I could contact on your behalf. You won't believe the amount of people who are on the streets here just because they can't afford the bus fare home and they're ashamed of admitting to their families what's happened to them. So if I could reconcile you with your family through phone contact, then we would pay for your bus fare home.'

'And if that didn't work? If, say, I was from London anyway, no family, all my friends are homeless as well, I've got nothing and nowhere to go back to – what then?'

'The next step would be to put you in touch with one of the hostels or charities: St Mungo's, Anchor House, The Passage, The Connection at St Martin-in-the-Fields.'

'I've been hearing those names a lot. People tell me I should visit them.'

'They're right. These are the places on the front line. The work they do is superb. The Connection's just around the corner from here – go and see them now.'

Acknowledging the implication in the imperative, I thanked my interlocutor for his time and left Charing Cross. The Connection was closed for the day, and when I contacted the other names I had heard so often – St Mungo's, Anchor House – I was informed that unless I was genuinely homeless I would have to make an appointment. That seemed fair, and I did.

8

St Mungo's in Camden was one of a number of hostels and housing projects the charity has across London and the South. With full disclosure of the purpose of my visit, I had arranged to meet a member of staff, who did not wish to be named, at the entrance for a tour and a chat.

'Thanks for this,' I said as we entered through the large doors. 'I thought about lying, trying to get in by saying I needed a bed for the night. But that would have been wrong. I would have taken a bed I don't need from someone who does.'

'Good call,' she smiled. 'We would have found you out anyway.'

Like the Compass Centre in Bristol, which St Mungo's also managed, the reception area was large, open, cool and comfortable. The hostel had been converted from an old Victorian school, and light beamed into the reception through the gigantic arched windows. Some of the residents sat around coffee tables in earnest conversation with their staff liaisons, a television played the muted and subtitled news in a corner, and every wall was plastered with posters advertising cooking groups, drop-in sessions, job opportunities, budgeting workshops, education and training possibilities, a walking club, a garden club and myriad others, all of which holistically promoted a clear agenda of health and well-being.

'All these options and opportunities are amazing,' I said. 'Do you think that, as long as a homeless person wants it enough, there are enough provisions available for them to successfully reintegrate?'

'There are services, and lots of them,' she replied. 'But each person is an individual and ideally you're offering the service they specifically need. And we don't say "reintegrate". We would say "rebuild".'

Language was important here. The residents were 'clients'. This was not a refuge or shelter but a 'hostel'. I liked that.

With my background in teaching, I knew all too well the importance of well-chosen words.

This St Mungo's hostel took people in who had a Camden connection. Its fifty-two beds were almost always full as people moved in and moved on. The reception area alone bustled with life as staff members and clients streamed through the doors.

'Where's Steve? *Steve*!' a man in his thirties hollered from the desk as he spun in distressed circles.

Steve appeared. 'What's up, Kyle?' he asked, walking towards him. 'Are you back?'

'No, mate, no. I just really need a talk.'

'Then let's talk.'

As Steve guided Kyle from the reception area, Kyle's nervous anxiety transformed into a calm smile. 'Thanks, mate,' he said.

'Any time,' Steve replied, and they disappeared behind closed doors.

I turned back to my guide, who was explaining that part of the hostel's current action plan was a focus on women in need. 'At the moment, a quarter of our clients are female.'

'That seems a lot. Of all the homeless people I've met on my journey, perhaps five per cent of them were female.'

'That could well be. In London around one in ten rough sleepers are women. Our residents aren't all rough sleepers, though. Just over half have slept rough but others are people with a mix of housing support needs, including people with mental health issues or who have found themselves victims of domestic abuse or troubled family relationships. What were the women you met like?'

'Sue wasn't that old, but she looked it. And I don't know for sure, but I think Tanya was a prostitute.'

My guide nodded. 'Of our women clients who have slept rough, around four in ten have been involved in prostitution. And, as for Sue, if she's spent enough time on the streets, regardless of how old she looks, there's a high likelihood that she has been raped at least once.'

The boldness of the assertion made me wince, and my guide must have noticed, for she went on to explain that, through extensive discussion with their clients, the staff at St Mungo's had ascertained that it was generally far more difficult for women on the streets than it was for men. Abuse and exploitation – both physical and mental – were commonplace, and this was compounded by the fact that most homelessness services in London and the rest of the UK have traditionally been set up for men.

'So what steps do you take to help these women who find themselves at your doors to rebuild?' I asked.

'The same steps we take with all our clients, men and women. But we're trying to be more aware of what particular needs women might have, maybe around sexual or domestic abuse or loss of contact with children.'

She explained that clients were able to stay at the hostel if they had some connection with Camden: either they were previously Camden residents or had a family connection within the borough. Some were referred to St Mungo's by outreach teams or Camden Council Housing, while others might come from referrals from the No Second Night Out hub, a twenty-four-hour assessment centre in Islington set up as the first port of call for new rough sleepers under the

NSNO scheme. At the hub, anyone who was newly rough sleeping was assessed on what led them to become homeless and, depending on what help they needed, was then referred into a hostel, private rented housing, a reconnection service depending on their visa status in the UK, or even into hospital. The first step, much like at the Charing Cross Homeless Unit, was to ascertain whether or not they had connections: friends or family who they might be comfortable returning to. If so, temporary accommodation and a bus or plane ticket home were paid for.

'I've read about people who were so embarrassed about the state they had ended up in that they didn't want to admit it to any authorities who might be able to help them,' I said.

'That's something outreach teams come across quite a lot, especially with people from Eastern European countries, people who've come over as migrant workers,' she replied. 'One man I met had come to London to work as a builder. He'd done well while the construction project was going, and was making enough to live and send a sizeable portion back home to his family each month. But then the project finished and he was let go. It wasn't so much that his family expected the money, it was more that he was too ashamed to admit to them that things weren't going well and he wasn't able to help them. It wasn't long before he exhausted his money, so he had to leave his flat, and rather than appeal to his family for support – in his mind, *he* was the one who gave support to *them* – he broke off contact and started living on the streets.'

For some people, it was not possible to return to families – they might have been the problem in the first place – or there might have been significant psychological problems which meant supported housing was needed.

'That doesn't mean that people always *want* to stay with us, though,' my guide said. 'Our main focus is recovery, and we do that with the offer of accommodation and support. But for those with unresolved psychological issues, coming here can be a step they don't want to take.'

I thought of Stan, of his refusal to enter the channels available to him because, in his mind, they would only serve to limit the few enjoyments he believed he had left. His chosen style of life corroborated what my guide told me: that stepping out of society and sleeping rough could in fact lend an inimitable freedom to one's life, with no responsibilities save those base necessities which ensured survival. Stepping off the streets and into a hostel meant tackling the problems which led one into homelessness in the first place and, for many, that could be too much to bear. Recently, the staff at St Mungo's had conducted a survey amongst rough sleepers and their residents about their sense of well-being, and had discovered that some rough sleepers rated themselves as feeling better than people within hostels.

'That's kind of understandable when you think about it,' my guide said. 'If people are in a really distressing situation, rough sleeping can be an opt-out solution, a way of leaving problems behind. Then, all you have to concentrate on are the basics: keeping warm, eating, staying safe, staying alive.'

Keeping warm had been one of my biggest preoccupations since leaving Sennen. Eating had not, for I had a stove and mess tins and cans of beans and enough money to buy more when I needed them. But what if I did not? That – pure sustenance – was surely the fundamental difficulty of living and sleeping rough. I asked my guide how anybody coped with the problem.

'I don't know what it's like in the rest of the country, but here in London there's soup runs, there's cafes and supermarkets which throw away unbought stock at the end of the day, there's people who will be generous and buy you a sandwich or a cup of tea. As long as you're not picky, you can find enough to sustain yourself. I'm not saying it's easy on the streets – it definitely isn't, of course – but it can be possible to survive.'

Once the rough sleeper entered a hostel and committed to it, however, new issues arose which may have lain redundant for years: seeing the doctor, managing benefits, getting on with the person next door, looking for jobs, *working* at those jobs, managing rent when you got rehoused, your utilities bills, managing your *life*. These were things that most people took for granted. But for those who had not had to deal with them for, say, the past five years, they were complicated and they were tough to assimilate.

'Plus, perhaps the hardest thing of all,' my guide continued, 'when you enter a hostel you are acknowledging that there's a problem, and even that you need support tackling it. There can be sometimes a "revolving door" where clients come but can't settle and end up back on the streets. Tackling your demons can be hard.'

I looked about the reception area at the dozen clients sat there. 'But some manage it,' I said.

'Some *do* manage it,' she replied, 'when they're given the chance, when others don't give up on them. We try and make St

Mungo's hostels places where you can be yourself, where people will tell you you're all right, where you can get your basics, your own space, where you can settle and start to be who you want to be. I know it doesn't sound like much, but it can be the start of a transformation. You have to start small and listen – it's only from there that you can help people rebuild their lives.'

This process of rebuilding, in terms of staying in a hostel, could take anything up to two years, and, in a Britain where many government-led initiatives focused on the quick fix, St Mungo's offered that time but also sought to move people on, rather than maintain or 'park' them.

We took a brief tour of the hostel's ground floor – the reception, the pool table, the quiet study areas behind floor-to-ceiling glass walls – ending at the outdoor smoking area.

'We do our best to offer support and assistance when nobody else does,' my guide said. '*Because* nobody else does. It's about safety nets. If one of the four per cent of our clients who works is sacked because they didn't show up for work for three days, the last thing they need is someone else telling them they've screwed up and they've got no place here, either. How would that help? We'd try and work out what happened, what led to them not showing up, and how we could help them salvage something. Rebuilding is not easy, no matter who you are. But you cannot do it *for* people. The last thing we want to do is institutionalise people, make them dependent on us. Like I said to you before, our main focus is recovery, and that means ultimately leaving here and going on to lead independent lives.'

She came to a halt and pointed towards a poster on the window which advertised cookery classes. 'See that? Pret a

Manger drop off any sandwiches to us that they have left over at the end of the day. As kind and generous as that is, you can't live on sandwiches all your life. So cookery classes are all about helping people to learn or relearn the skills which will make them self-sufficient, capable. It comes down to our recovery approach – *everyone* should have a decent place to live, enjoy good health, have something meaningful to do, and also have satisfying relationships.'

Two men came through the door to appear out in the smoking area. The first, Alan, was a hostel resident; the second, Matthew, was a friend who did not stay at the hostel but who came regularly to offer support and encouragement to Alan. Alan clocked me immediately.

'What's your name?' he said. When he spoke, he leaned forward with his head but not his body, and his pupils darted with a firm focus from my left eye to my right and then back to my left again. He had dirty teeth and a dirtier cap, thin legs, and a bulge around his midriff which looked like he was concealing a football beneath his coat.

'Charlie,' I replied, offering him my hand.

'What do you do?'

'I'm a writer.'

Alan's eyes widened. 'I'm a writer, too.'

'What are you writing?' I asked.

'Leave him alone, Alan,' Matthew called from the seat he had taken. 'Come and have a fag with me.'

'He's a writer, Matthew,' Alan said without turning around to look at him. 'I'm telling him about my book. He's fascinated, look.'

Matthew leaned back and sighed. 'Go on, then.'

'It's real crime,' Alan said, staring at me intensely. 'About the Clerkenwell murder.'

'What's that?'

'What's that, he asks! I'll tell you.' And he did, though with such rapidity that I found it hard to keep up. It involved a case he had intimate and personal knowledge of, and he assured me he had cracked it. 'Next month, I'm starting a computer course. Then I'll write my novel. I'll let you know when I launch it.'

'Do,' I urged.

'There's more I could tell you. I used to work at the Palace. I know all about what happened to Di. She ripped them all right off.'

'Come on, Alan,' Matthew remonstrated. 'I'm here to see you. We were going to talk about getting you into a new place. You don't want to live here all your life, do you?'

'No, mate, I won't, I'm just having a chat,' Alan implored.

'I mean, it's nice enough here.' Matthew looked at me, gestured towards the tall windows, and then turned back to face Alan. 'But you need to move on with your life.'

'Diamond, he is,' Alan said, nodding at his friend. 'How long we known each other, Matthew?'

'Forty years.'

'*Forty* years,' Alan repeated. 'Diamond.' He shook my hand again and walked towards his friend. Matthew lit a cigarette for him. It was all part of the St Mungo's philosophy: support by whatever means, helping the client feel valued again. Alan, I thought, was lucky to have a friend like Matthew, a regular visitor who gave him personal and frequent encouragement to rebuild his life. It was a boon I suspected the staff at St

Mungo's wished upon all their clients. As I left the smoking area, and St Mungo's with it, I heard Matthew say to his friend: 'Now, tell me about your computer course. That sounds good...'

9

It's all right, I thought as one night in the London house morphed into two and two into four and four into an entire week. *I'm not paying, I'm couch-surfing. Tramps do this all the time. For as long as their friends will let them.*

I was fortunate that my friends were good friends and would have let me stay for as long as I wanted. But as much as I helped with the washing-up and did my best to keep out of their way, rising and showering in the morning long before they needed the bathroom to prepare themselves for an honourable day of work while I skulked and roamed about the city with my knapsack on and my hood up, an unerring sense of guilt pervaded. How long could a tramp take advantage of a friend's hospitality in this way before the friendship was ruined? Perhaps some waited until the last moment. I would not.

Seven days passed, and in that time the conversational exchanges grew shorter, the novelty diminished, the cooked dinners and proffered pints at the local pub dissipated, the smell of my clothes intensified, and I knew I was risking things. One of my friends was a teacher, and when she returned home to work further hours planning and marking, the guilt I felt at taking up her couch after her long days of pursuing a profession I had dropped out of to tramp became insurmountable. She, of course, betraying the saintliness of most teachers, never said a word, but I knew full well how I would feel if some scrounging, stinking freeloader slept on my couch each night without offering to pay a penny while I worked a difficult job each day to make ends meet.

As I left the St Mungo's hostel, I resolved that the coming night would be my last at the house, that it was time for me to learn London from the rough sleeper's perspective. I still had no clue where I might spend my nights, but less fear surrounded the prospect than it had when I walked beneath the M25. Tramping London's streets over the last seven daytimes had bred a semblance of familiarity with them, and the visit to St Mungo's had helped, too: the homeless people it took in had slept rough in London, and had survived it.

I reflected further on St Mungo's as I walked back to Hackney. It was a far cry from Orwell's spikes of almost a hundred years ago: with their iron gates; tiny, barred windows; the ambience of, at best, a blacking warehouse and, at worst, a prison; stone cells; two bathtubs and one towel; chamber pots; a thick wedge of buttered bread and a cup of cocoa for dinner and breakfast. St Mungo's, on the other hand, was modern, it was efficient, and it was worthy. Between all the St Mungo's hostels and all the staff who worked at them, they had helped thousands off the streets and back into houses, back into work, back into life. I was about to take the opposite trajectory – out of a London house, and on to London streets.

CHAPTER SEVEN

LONDON STREETS

I

I walked away from the house and followed Kingsland Road south towards the river, through Shoreditch and along Bishopsgate, turning right at Monument and then heading west past St Paul's and along Fleet Street. It took hours, for I stopped every few metres to investigate alleyways and alcoves, entrances and exits: the dark spaces of Central London hidden in and amongst the thin tributaries of the city's throbbing pedestrian network. Most were too well lit, too noisy and too noticeable for the secluded anonymity I craved, and the few spots which met my vague criteria, which seemed likely, were already earmarked by the telltale signs of a mattress or sleeping bag. Almost all of the latter, I noticed, were behind wheelie-bins, enveloped by the necrotic odours of rotting litter. It was not the smell which put me off these places, but the potential for hand-to-hand turf wars.

I joined the Strand after dark. Though it was growing late, there were few rough sleepers, outnumbered by the plethora of businessmen who clustered outside bars drinking from wine glasses and ranting into their phones, lit by the ethereal glow from the night-time Royal Courts of Justice. One homeless man begged helplessly at a junction, offering a hostile nod as I passed, and two others wandered with slow and curving footsteps, perhaps waiting for the employed to leave so they could bed down amongst the orange bin bags.

As the road progressed towards Charing Cross and its street lighting grew stronger, the homeless increased in number – some solitary, others in pairs or groups, some with dogs, some with cardboard cups of takeaway coffee, underneath cash machines and outside restaurants, the repeated refrain 'Spare some change please' not so much a question as a needful command.

I walked on to Trafalgar Square. What was it that made me keep coming back here? Orwell, probably. I remembered the *Clergyman's Daughter* scene as I waited at the pedestrian crossing for the green man to appear. Perhaps I would find my Deafie, my Mrs Bendigo and my Mr Tallboys here. Perhaps I could be their Charlie.

It was possible: the square at night was an emaciated counterpart to the square at day, but life flickered across it with a brave appreciation for the midnight shadows and empty flagstones. A Louis Armstrong impressionist crooned over an amplified backing track to the tipsy delight of his small audience, who clapped at the close of each song with gloved hands, lo-fi approval for the lo-fi performance. Behind him, bodies lay sprawled across the small patch of lawn in front of the National Gallery's east wing. I moved softly amongst them: young American and European backpackers sharing bottles of white wine in disposable cups; kissing couples, many same-sex; one middle-aged man with his duffel coat undone to reveal a suit beneath, his eyes a revelation of heartbreak and loss. In a corner, eight rough sleepers lay in a tangle beneath a web of sleeping bags. They had their backs to everybody else and, when the crooner stopped between songs, they were the only ones who did not applaud.

I found space beside the wall of the National Gallery's steps and settled there, untying my sleeping bag from my knapsack and shrouding myself in it, sat up with my knees to my chin and my back to the wall. I was paid no attention, and this pleased me. As the hours passed, the couples, the crooner and the backpackers slowly filtered away into the streets. The duffel coat was the last to leave, though his departure followed a haphazard trajectory which took him to the foot of Nelson's Column, around a lion, and then to the lip of one of the shallow pools, which he leaned over, using his hips as a pivot so that his feet left the ground and his face dangled over the water. I readied myself to spring should he attempt a half-hearted and ludicrous suicide in the foot of water, but he righted himself again and drifted away towards Admiralty Arch.

Traffic diminished, and Trafalgar Square became as quiet as it perhaps ever was. Mumbles and the occasional fart percolated out from the web of sleeping bags, sometimes succeeded by an arm, leg or hooded head. I remained sat upright, and I did not sleep.

2

Frank was in his early fifties: gaunt, toothless, four thick black hairs sprouting from the bridge of his nose. I bought a *Big Issue* from him at his regular pitch in Covent Garden.

'I've been on the streets on and off for about twenty of the last forty years. I got these headaches. I didn't know why they came and I couldn't control them. Killers, they were. And they always happened when I was getting settled back into housing. So I would go back on the streets, and they would stop. After a while, I thought I'd got them licked, and would try getting housed. Sure enough, the moment I had myself settled in a place, the headaches would start again.'

'Migraines?' I asked.

'Much, much worse than that. I used to get migraines when I was a kid, so I know what they're like. These ones, though, they were damning.'

I noticed he was speaking in the past tense, and asked if he had managed to find a cure.

'Not a cure, but I've finally got them diagnosed. Imagine that! Forty years of the killers, and they've only just worked out what they are. Some people call them "suicide headaches". You ever heard of them?'

I admitted I had not.

'They're like a metronome. Three months off and then three months on with up to three a day. So regular and so bad some people just kill themselves to get rid. That's their cure. Suicide. Not me, though. You wouldn't catch me doing that, no matter how bad things got.'

Forty years of headaches so bad they make you want to kill yourself, I thought.

'The thing about them is they're caused by a lack of oxygen in the blood. And, for me, they seemed to come on worse when I was inside – less oxygen there, see? – and they got better when I was back outside. So I got to thinking I must just be a square peg in a round hole. Everyone else is on the streets because of addictions, but I'm actually *healthier* here. Funny. But now they've finally diagnosed. Took forty years of doctors, but they've done it in the end. I know how to control it now, nothing more than a little tank of oxygen. Doctor says when they come on I just go in and they'll give me one. It's been three months without. I'm due any day now. I'm almost looking forward to it, cos I can just go in and get my tank. *Then* I'll be off the streets for good.'

Frank's story was rare on the streets, for it was an uplifting one. Someone stopped beside us to buy a *Big Issue* and I left Frank to resume his business. 'Any day now!' he gleefully hollered to me as I bid him farewell. 'Can you believe it? I'm actually *looking forward* to my next headache!'

3

I did not want to spend another night on Trafalgar Square. There had been no trouble there, but there had also been no sleep, and I felt the urge to close my eyes so acutely the following day that I wondered if I should risk a more dangerous location in the hope of gaining a few hours' rest.

Perhaps the nights on that Dalston couch in that quiet and heated living room had spoiled me, but I had slept rough over the past months enough times to know what it was I needed. A space. A space which I could stick my metaphorical flag into and claim as my own, no matter how temporarily. I had no sense of that on Trafalgar Square; everything was too fluid, too open. There was no demarcation, no feasible notion that someone might point to where I had sat through the night and say: 'That's where Charlie sleeps.' I knew I would never find anywhere like my woods in Bristol, my sand dunes and cliff-tops in Cornwall, my canal-side pitches – nothing like that existed in Central London. But I had seen mattresses and duvets all around the city. They had not been discarded: they were makeshift bedrooms. That was what I wanted. Somewhere I could leave my sleeping bag.

The nesting instinct, I thought, *as basic as an insect*. Rough sleepers have little, but territoriality comes before thought, is reactive, and ignoring it is as impossible as denying vision. It is pure self-preservation – never are you more vulnerable than when you are asleep, and if you feel vulnerable, you will not sleep – and so all tramps, like all nomads, will have defined spots they return to again and again when night falls.

That was my problem. I had felt vulnerable on Trafalgar Square. And I had not slept. I thought back over my time thus far in London, trying to recall any locations where I might feel secure enough to sleep. I remembered the conversation with Tim of the London House and his allusion to a new Cardboard City. It was worth looking into. I set off for the Hammersmith Flyover.

Driving from the West Country to London over the past decade, I had crossed the Hammersmith Flyover scores of times. Emerging from the shopping arcade into the dull light drifting down the sides of the road's legs, I recognised it with its Apollo Theatre and digital billboards. I never knew that this was the Hammersmith Flyover; for me, in my car, van or bus, it had been London's west gate, as familiar a watershed as Paddington Station.

Beyond the pedestrian crossing, I walked beneath the gigantic totem to civil engineering from one end to the next. There was no Cardboard City. Aside from a car park, all available space beneath that thunderous shelter was subsumed by the jackhammers, portable fences, hi-vis jackets and dust of the Conway construction company.

'What are they working on?' I asked a fellow pedestrian.

'Who?' she replied.

Though she passed the fences so close she could reach out to touch them, she had, it seemed, not noticed. And why would she? London itself could often feel like one huge construction site in perpetuity.

I began to ask each person I crossed paths with about Cardboard City. The range of answers was non-committal and contradictory.

'A cardboard *city*? Nope. Never been one.'

'Sure, it's still down at the eastern end.' (It wasn't.)

'Used to be, but they *had* to move it. There's a primary school right there.' He pointed at the St Paul's CE Primary School, which competed against the motor-noise of the flyover with its playground yells and screams of tiny children. He shrugged his shoulders and moved on. I wondered if he had confused the words 'homeless' and 'paedophile'.

'I've never seen a cardboard city,' another said. 'And I've been coming here for *months*.'

Only one person asked me why I wanted to know. I explained myself. She told me to follow her. 'It's all right,' she said, 'I'm going this way anyway.'

We walked back towards the Apollo Theatre, keeping beneath the flyover whenever possible. She stopped momentarily and pointed at one of the pillars. 'Have you seen that?'

I followed the line of her finger. On the pillar, beneath a cracked 'CCTV in operation' sign was the red, block-capitalised proclamation: 'BILL STICKERS WILL BE PROSECUTED.' Below that, someone had graffitied 'Bill Stickers is innocent!'

The woman chuckled. 'That's good, that is.'

We continued on our way to the far end of the flyover, and I asked her if she knew what the Conway workforce were doing.

'They've been here ages. I don't think they're doing anything. Just keeping the homeless from coming back.'

'So there used to be homeless here?'

'Used to be. Now there's just one young couple. I give them money sometimes. I'll introduce you. They're nice.'

She led me on to the western tip, where the flyover slowly begins to descend over the busy A306. There, the far perimeter of the Conway fencing pushed up a few feet away from the final pillar, and nestled between the two was a tiny habitation.

'They're not in,' my guide said, peering over its walls. 'Odd, they're usually around at this time. Wait a bit and they'll probably come back. I can't stay.'

The habitation was chest-height, its four walls each composed of different materials: at the back, the concrete pillar, then a wooden pallet on one side and cardboard boxes on another, and at the front a sheet of plywood which was clearly moved back and forth as a makeshift door. Between them, they comprised the exact dimensions of a double mattress, and I imagined there must have been one beneath the pile of coverless and filthy duvets.

I waited there for some time, but the homeless couple did not return. To compensate, I allowed myself a brief inspection of their dwelling. Old and knackered suitcases served as ballast for the walls, propping them upright, and on top of them a carefully constructed stack of empty cider cans formed a fortress-like impression. Crushed cigarette packets littered the bed alongside a wind-up torch, torn and empty crisp bags, and a half-empty jar of Marmite. A small rucksack, zipped shut, lay in the corner, beside it a transparent bottle of fizzy pop filled with a dark liquid which was either brown or yellow depending on the angle I looked at it. Around that was scattered a mess of tiny glass bottles with their labels removed.

I walked one final length. At the eastern dip, a courthouse stood back from the road. Before leaving, I decided to hazard one final attempt at discovering whether or not there had ever been a Cardboard City here, and stepped inside.

Two security guards, with their thin stubble and thick East African accents, sat behind the reception desk. A fat and bald policeman, his voice as resounding and Cockney as, I imagined, his grandmother's, leaned over the desk and cracked one-liners. Their conversation stopped as I approached.

'Help you?' one of the guards asked.

The policeman shifted his hips so that his bulk faced me.

'Was there ever a Cardboard City here, under the flyover?' I asked.

'Why?' the policeman drawled.

'I'm doing some research into homelessness.'

'Research, eh?' He stared at me for a few uncomfortable seconds, then turned back to face the guards and rested his chin on an open palm. He did not speak again, but listened.

'Cardboard City,' the guard mused. 'Let me think.' He spoke quickly but carefully, the intonation of a stutterer who has overcome his impediment. 'There used to be a Cardboard City here. But that was a long time ago. How long have I been working here? It was... erm... two years... yes, two years ago they cleared it. Had to for the roadworks.'

But this was not Conway. The original company had been there for a brief resurfacing project. When they finished, the homeless moved back.

'Not for long,' the guard continued. 'These lot came in straight after and chased them all away again.'

'How long have Conway been here?' I asked.

'Who?'

'Conway. The construction company out there now.'

'Seems like forever.' He laughed, and the other guard laughed with him. The policeman did not.

It was scant information, but it revealed one thing. Beneath Hammersmith Flyover, permanence was the issue: a fear of homeless permanence replaced by construction permanence. There were no more cardboard boxes; no more wafts of alcohol or recycled fag-smoke; no more incomprehensible roadside ranting or belligerent begging. Instead, there was the never-ending staccato of the jackhammer; the bellows not of a drunken or distressed rough sleeper, but the banter of shouting workmen; and the derangement of high-decibel noise pollution. No one seemed to know how long Conway would stay, or what they were even there for. But they were tolerated nonetheless, one public nuisance in place of another.

4

It was clear that I could not spend the night beneath the Hammersmith Flyover. Feeling the ache of miles of walking on a lone sandwich and no sleep in the last twenty-four hours, I trudged sullenly back towards the Strand and Fleet Street, remembering the policeman I had met on Trafalgar Square on the day of the Paralympic Games celebration. He had suggested this long stretch of road as an emergency venue for new rough sleepers, and I was beginning to feel that I could readily pass out anywhere upon it, regardless of who I might meet.

But first I needed to eat. The policeman had also said that there was a soup kitchen near Charing Cross Police Station. I stopped the first homeless person I met on Belgrave Square and asked if he knew about it.

'Soup *kitchen*?' he spat. 'No fucking *kitchens* round here. There's a soup *run* outside Zimbabwe House. *Run*, mate, *run*.'

The distinction between noun and imperative was unclear to me. The man laughed, and whether or not it was spiteful was also unclear. I needed to eat. I needed to sleep.

'What time is it?' he spat. He seemed to have no other mode of verbalisation.

'Half seven,' I said, checking my digital watch.

'You'll make it, no prob. Don't usually serve till gone ten.' He laughed again.

Much later – gone ten, in fact – I decided the laugh was spiteful. I arrived outside Zimbabwe House on the Strand at eight o'clock, gratified to see the large congregation of homeless there milling about the cobbled space, perched on shop windowsills or slumped on the ground. They were clearly waiting for something.

By nine o'clock, that something had still not arrived, and though I knew I had another hour to wait, I noticed that the crowd had not increased but had in fact diminished. Two six-strong groups of Eastern Europeans had come to dominate the small area, circling around and then facing off against each other in what appeared to be some weird *West Side Story* love-and-revenge melodrama. One woman ran back and forth between the two groups, wailing her invectives and stoking the flames, appearing to be simultaneously on both sides and neither, until a young man heeded her screeches and stepped forward into the no-man's-land between the two packs. Within a second, another young man from the opposite group rushed out to meet him with a punch to the face. The first man swayed and fell to the floor as the second man kicked him in the gut, and then the woman's screams rose even higher in pitch at the fallen victim. He brought himself back to his feet, wavered once, and returned to his group. The argument continued.

The rest of us stood at the periphery, bags dangling from hands, watching with no intention of intervention. The man closest to me, sucking hard on a roll-up as fat and wet as a slug, nudged me with his shoulder. 'Feckin' pikeys,' he laughed, blowing smoke into my face.

'Where's the soup run?' I asked. 'Did I miss it?'

'What?'

'The soup run? Has it already been here?'

He laughed and nodded. 'Feckin' pikeys,' he said again. 'Always at it.'

I realised he was profoundly deaf.

'Lom,' he said, holding out his hand.

'Lom? That's your name?'

He looked bewildered, then laughed again. 'Lom,' he repeated. 'What's your name?'

'Charlie,' I said. 'How long have you been homeless, Lom?'

He laughed once more. 'Watch the pikeys. Who needs telly?'

By ten o'clock, the two groups disappeared in opposite directions along the Strand. By half past, the rest of the homeless followed, leaving me alone outside Zimbabwe House. Dinner had been served long ago, I realised. That laugh *was* spiteful.

I had never felt so hungry, nor so tired. I was cold, too, but that barely registered. I needed to eat and I needed to sleep. Not far from Zimbabwe House, I pushed my way through the throngs of wine-quaffing businessmen who had filled the still air with cigarette smoke and down a small alleyway. I saw two wheelie-bins and, behind that, the requisite sleeping bag. I did not care any longer. I pulled a tin of beans and sausages from the bottom of my knapsack and wrenched it open with my bending penknife, eating it cold with my plastic spork. I could have cooked the food in a mess tin on my tiny stove, but I was too impatient. I would have happily spooned the meal into my mouth with my fingers.

My dinner over, I cast the empty tin into one of the wheelie-bins, licked the spork clean before placing it back in my knapsack, and crawled into my sleeping bag. To close my eyes and surrender to the all-consuming exhaustion which had nagged at me throughout the day was perhaps the most blissful sensation on the whole journey so far. Spread long on the concrete, my knapsack beneath my head, I opened one eye and could see that I was in full view of eleven or twelve men who stood outside the pub. Even that didn't matter any more.

5

The first thing which came to mind was that the kick was not so much a kick, more a gentle nudge. Consciousness was immediate, and I even had time to make the decision whether or not to open my eyes. I chose to do so.

'Can't sleep here,' the man towering over me said.

'Fuck it,' I grumbled, closing my eyes again – another conscious decision. 'There's room for everybody.'

'No,' the man said. 'No, there ain't.' He kicked me again, this time slightly harder. 'This place is mine. I ain't sharing tonight.'

I sat up quickly. I had thought it was someone from the pub, or maybe even the police, but understanding that this was the owner of the sleeping bag transformed my blasé attitude into fear in an instant.

'Sorry, mate, sorry,' I blathered. 'I'm just... sorry, mate... I didn't know where else to go.'

'Go where you want,' he said, seeming satisfied enough with my reaction to begin stepping into his own sleeping bag. 'Just not here.'

I jumped to my feet and began to bundle my gear beneath my arm. 'Sorry,' I said again. 'I'm new here.' But he was no longer looking at me, was already tying the hood of his sleeping bag around his head and squirming into a foetal position.

I felt suddenly preposterous. What claim did this man have to this small patch of concrete? Why *couldn't* I sleep here? I fancied kicking him in the ribs, see how he liked it.

I stood there for a while, unsure what to do. The man ignored me.

'I don't know where to go,' I finally said.

'Go where you want. Somewhere else.'

A glass smashed somewhere behind us. A drunken cheer rose from the outdoor smokers.

'*Sake*!' the man announced from the folds of his sleeping bag, before sitting up with his back against the bin, pulling the hood down around his neck and looking at me. He was younger than me, I realised, much younger. Perhaps only just twenty. A light and ginger stubble grew around his upper lip but nowhere else on his face, and the high cheekbones which would have made him pretty in a catalogue made him sinister in the refracted light from the nearby pub. He was lean and wiry, and looked the kind to scratch and bite you in a fight if it came to it. I was glad I had not kicked him.

'You need to fuck off,' he said. 'I'm done in.'

'Where?'

'I don't know, somewhere on the Strand?'

'I'll do that, and someone else will kick me in the ribs while I'm sleeping and tell me to fuck off.'

'The Strand's not like that. It's like a queue. They sleep in a line up there. Find a gap in the line and it's yours. You'll have it for as long as you want. I don't like it there. Too busy. But if you can handle all the feet you can lie there twenty-four-seven.'

'Thanks,' I said.

'You got a fag?'

'No.'

'Any food?'

I reached into my knapsack and produced a cereal bar. He snatched it from my outstretched hand and tore it open.

'I missed the soup run today,' I said. 'What time should I get there tomorrow?'

'This time of year,' he replied with a mouthful of cereal bar, 'between five and seven.'

I pushed my way back through the crowd of drinkers and up on to the Strand. Walking its length once I could see what my interlocutor had meant: the rough sleepers did indeed form a kind of line which was perceptible if you looked for it. Each was alone, and there was never less than twenty feet of space between a head and the next pair of feet. Finding a gap in the line was easy, there were many along the street, and I made sure to observe the invisible demarcations between me and my closest neighbours.

An hour passed before I was able to fall asleep again, but when I did I stayed comatose until almost six in the morning. I awoke to the feet. Already, the Strand's pavement was a motorway of pedestrians who hurried in both directions, impatient but careful to make no physical contact with each other or, I noticed, with any of us rough sleepers. A foot-wide no-man's-land flanked me, and none ever stepped into it nor even looked down to check that which they skirted. I turned on my side, pulled the sleeping bag tighter around my body, and watched the river of boots, wedges and black shoes as it flowed ceaselessly past my ground-level eyes.

6

Jane sat begging with her back against a tree and her bare legs open. It was rare to see a woman on the streets but, as Jane explained, 'I can look after meself'. She looked like she could and, with her deep Midlands voice, I briefly wondered if she was, under all that padding, male.

'Cheers for this, love,' she said when I gave her a pound. 'Last bloke gave me a penny. I threw it back at him and told him to fuck off. Better dressed than *you* he was, too.'

She was sixty-two, though she looked younger. That was another rarity on the streets. Homelessness aged people perceptibly.

'It all depends on how you take care of yourself,' she said. 'And I *do*.' She made a fist. 'What do you think of that bloke with the penny, though, eh?'

'Taking the piss,' I said.

'It *is* taking the piss. I fucking hate it when they give me coppers. *I* don't want them. It's like all those foreigners coming over here and taking English jobs. Taking the piss. *I* don't want them.'

Oh, no.

'I have to go now, Jane,' I said, and walked away.

7

Many equate busking with begging. They are wrong. Accuse a busker of begging and he may wrap his guitar around your ribs. There is a stock phrase many buskers use at the close of a 'set', one which I have used myself many times:

Thank you for listening/watching, ladies and gentlemen. And please remember, I'm trying to make a living, not a phone call.

Buskers *earn*. That's what we'll tell you. We provide entertainment. And if you feel that entertainment deserves recognition, financial compensation, then so much the better. I never made enough to live from busking, but I knew, and still know, some who do. Busking is an *al fresco* alternative to the pub gig, the circus act or the spoken-word event. An 'Open Mic' in the afternoon. A street sideshow. A performance.

Nevertheless, busking grew from begging as a subsidiary legal loophole. Until as late as the first half of the twentieth century, Britain's vagrancy laws could condemn a man to seven days in jail for openly begging. But if that man were to belt out an *a capella* song while he walked the streets with his hand out, he was deemed to be in pursuit of a legitimate trade. Many beggars would carry with them a tray of loose matches to sell or a stick of chalk with which to etch an impromptu picture on the ground should a policeman approach.

Today, begging is perfectly legal and, with this in mind, I walked to Aldwych and sat on the pavement opposite Australia House, crossing my legs and placing my cap on the concrete before me. Begging was not a statutory requirement of being homeless – Stan once told me he had never begged a penny in his life – but I wanted an insider's perspective on as many of the tramp's experiences as I could, and one of those was to become a beggar.

The first ten minutes were humiliating and they were demeaning. Visible poverty was, as Orwell once noted, spiritual halitosis. But the shame exhausted itself quickly. I began to look up, to search for eye contact with the myriad passers-by. Some looked at me with pity, others with hostility, and still others with a palpable fear. But most ignored me. Begging on the street, I attained an invisibility comparable only to that I had experienced when I awoke on the Strand that morning. It is this ignorance which hurts the beggar most, and it makes the few acknowledgements one receives almost too tender to bear. Four people stopped to give me money, each of a different character: a forty-year-old man in a suit who looked away as he dropped a pound coin at my feet; a woman who implored I 'spend this on food'; an old Indian man who passed me three times and then insisted on placing a fifty-pence piece in my palm rather than my hat; and a girl whose smile was shy but lovely. 'You're *very* welcome,' she said when I thanked her.

Just as wonderful as these kind donors were the three who gave me a warm and caring smile. I felt inordinate gratitude for all seven of these people: they had no need or reason to give me money or attention – who was I to them? Nobody! – but they did regardless, and the pure loveliness of that outweighed all the humiliation.

Rising to my feet and walking away, I found Frank, still at his pitch in Covent Garden. The long-anticipated headache which would be enough to send him to the doctor, who would give him the oxygen tank which symbolised the start of his new life, had not yet arrived.

'Good day?' I asked.

'No. Only shifted three.'

That was six pounds for a full day's work.

'Here,' I said, holding out the £3.25 I had begged.

'You sure?'

'I can't keep it.'

8

I arrived at Zimbabwe House in time for the soup run and was given a cheese roll, which I demolished in seconds. When the food was gone, three people left immediately, but the rest of the forty or so there remained. Some sat and talked, smoking roll-ups and drinking from cans, but most lingered quietly and alone. I wondered why, then realised that I was also one of the latter, and that I had not left, either.

What was the point? What else was there to do? We could all sit about here with nothing to do or return to our sleeping-spots and sit about there with nothing to do. Perhaps I should go for a walk, I thought, see some of London, warm up. There was money in my pocket. Maybe I could go to the cinema, or buy a decent meal, or sequester a table in a pub and drink pint after pint until last orders. But I barely had the energy to even choose between the options, to make any kind of concrete decision, and so I remained outside Zimbabwe House, daydreaming of my wife, of television, of a bottle of wine and of curtains.

I had left my sleeping bag at my spot on the Strand and, when I returned, it was still there, untouched. I realised I finally had my own pitch in London, my own bedroom, but the thought merely caused further depression, listlessness, demotivation and, below them all, the oncoming throbs of an insistent headache. Crawling into my sleeping bag, I turned my face to the wall and closed my eyes, drifting in and out of consciousness through a serial of dreamed and imagined dramas, through the windows of memories and the doors of sensation, through feverish emotion and wracking conundrums, all the while keeping my eyes closed, even when I cried.

Night passed and dawn brought the feet which rapped an urgent tattoo a foot away from my head. I lay still, face to the wall. A soft rain fell, dotting the tip of my nose and spreading a metallic odour across the flagstones. I lay still, face to the wall. A flash of sun became discernible through my closed eyelids; a burst of wind whipped and buffeted the sleeping bag about my legs. I lay still, face to the wall.

This was not life. It was barely even existence. Fatigue, boredom and longing wrestled with such strength and volume in my mind that to even begin to assess or evaluate, to decide or act, became mere trivialities. Until now, tramping had been exciting, romantic even, but here on the Strand I felt like I was waiting to die. And this was me, me with my safety net: enough money to buy a bus ticket home that day and return to my wife and house, where I could be warm and listen to music and mow the lawn and get fat.

The thought of the safety net speared my mind like caffeine, and I sat up, looking down the Strand queue. What if I didn't have that? I doubted that any of them had anything which came even close. How did they cope? How did any rough sleeper ever find the resources to pull themselves back up from this slow-frying rock bottom?

I stood up. My body trembled. I needed salt, sugar, a quick hit of something familiar and comforting, the greasier the better. I found a McDonald's, bought a Happy Meal, and ate it miserably.

9

The food squirmed in my stomach like a mound of writhing leeches, but walking it off made me feel better. *Walking* made me feel better. I met Don, who had been flogging his *Big Issue*s all morning and was ready for a break.

'I'm heading back to Victoria Street for a bit,' he said. 'You can come, if you like.'

'I've got nothing else to do.'

Like many others, Don slept on Victoria Street because of what he called all the 'free roofs': the hundreds of metres of concrete overhangs which pushed out from the shops, supported by stone pillars, creating an awning-esque shelter across the pavement.

We passed Victoria Station and the touch-screen information point which stood beside the pedestrian crossing. It was there for local rough sleepers, and its various pages gave information on where to stay at night, where to go during the day, and contact points for emergency help. Above the screen, in a gigantic font, were the words:

On the Right Track
Free 24 Hour Homeless Advice
THIS IS NOT TOURIST INFORMATION

Don pointed at it as we passed. 'Don't use that. Nobody uses that. It records your fingerprints. Then they know who you are.'

'How long have you been homeless?' I asked.

'Only eighteen months.'

'*Only*? A year and a half sounds like a long time to be on the streets.'

'Two winters isn't bad. Not compared to some of my mates. Here's them now.'

He stopped at the edge of Christchurch Gardens and nodded towards six men who clustered around a bench.

'Best we part company here,' Don said.

'Why?'

'You're not homeless, are you?'

'I'm sleeping rough.' I was about to tell him where, but something stopped me.

'Yeah, but you're not homeless. Are you?'

I laughed. 'What gave it away?'

'Your voice. And all the fucking questions.'

'Do you think they won't like me?'

'Some of them have been on the streets for over thirty years. Put it this way. They won't take to you.'

10

My journal on the grass beside me reminded me that I had a purpose. Hyde Park in the late afternoon on a cold October's day was quiet, and the acres of green, un-peopled space around me gave me succour. I cooked two cans of chicken soup in a mess tin on my stove, turned the heat down low and spooned away at the liquid while it bubbled, turning the pages of my journal with my free hand.

My journey from Sennen to here lay within the bullet points, sketches and mini-essays of my handwriting. When I had left Don at Christchurch Gardens and walked without aim until I found myself on the lip of Hyde Park, I had wondered whether it was time to go home. I was footsore and burned-out, exhausted and sullen, but seeing those blank pages at the back of my journal made me want to fill them. I had, I reasoned, only spent three nights thus far on the streets of

London. There was still more to do, more to experience and more to observe. If I could muster enough self-discipline to keep on my feet, to keep away from the seductive lure of that sleeping bag and its all-consuming darkness, I still had the time and the will to conclude this journey, and not simply run from it.

Two men with five children and a ball appeared from the edge of the lake, dropped their bags on to the grass at a respectable distance from me, and initiated a game which involved booting the ball as far away as possible and then shouting encouragement as the children raced after it. Once, it came my way, landing a few metres from my stove. I rose to my feet and kicked it back. 'Thank you!' one of the children called, trapping the ball between his legs as another, tinier child expertly tackled him and sent him plummeting to the ground. His giggles rose into the sky and drifted out over London.

||

When the feet woke me at seven in the morning, I wrenched off the sleeping bag, rolled it into a ball, sat upon it and ate a cereal bar. The feet seemed to have doubled in volume that morning – *what day is it?* I thought, and could not remember – and I lay my hat before me and tried the line I had heard so many times since arriving in London.

'Spare some change, please?'

It had no effect. Perhaps I wasn't saying it right.

'Spare some change *please*.'

Still nothing.

'Spare *some* change... please?'

I might as well have been petitioning the government.

I decided to focus on individuals.

'Spare a quid, mate?'

'Any spare change, love?'

But heads remained fixed, pointed towards the office and the day of work ahead. Perhaps it was me, my lack of conviction. I didn't need their change. Maybe they sensed that. I tried a different approach.

'Spare some books, please?'

Success. One man, jolted out of his composure by the non-standard request, looked briefly down at me. Eye contact. I continued.

'Anything to read, mate?'

He grinned nervously, said nothing, and continued walking. I tried again.

'Spare a book, please?... Poor and hungry to read... Down and out but not illiterate... Got a spare paperback?... Will work for Dickens.'

A pregnant woman with a rotund bulge distending out from her fitted jacket stopped, reached into her handbag and pulled out a copy of *The Independent*. 'Will this do?' she asked.

'You've saved a man's life,' I grinned, taking it from her hands. 'I'll read it today and use it for insulation tonight.'

Her smile faded at my tasteless joke and she hurried away. I wished I had not said it.

12

Ibrahim had no time for my questions.

'What do you mean, on the streets? I am not on the streets. I am a living man. I live. That is all.'

'Where do you sleep at night?'

'Everywhere. I sleep where I like. This does not mean I am on the streets. Where do you sleep at night?'

'On a couch,' I lied.

'And do you tell people you live on the couches?' He laughed loud and slapped his open hand against my shoulder, almost pushing me off the bench. 'You see the nonsense you speak?'

I laughed, too.

'You think I am homeless, don't you?' he said.

'Yes.'

'And why do you think this?'

I hesitated, unsure how to answer. It was because his hair was unwashed, his clothes were torn and dirty, he had a sleeping bag draped over his legs, a stained and bulging rucksack at his feet, and he was sitting on a bench eating chicken legs and watching the River Thames. But I didn't want to tell him that.

'It is because I *look* homeless, isn't it?' he said, anticipating my response before I could give it. Then he laughed again, dropping the chicken leg into the plastic tray. 'It is OK. I know what I look like.'

'So you're not homeless?'

'I am not homeless, and I am not-not-homeless. You see?'

'No.'

'What does it matter to you if I have a home? And what does it matter to *me* if I have a home? Here, eat this chicken.' He held a leg out to me.

'I'm all right, thanks. I've already had lunch.'

'Eat the fucking chicken. It's good meat.'

He waved it so close to my nose I took it, if only for fear that he was about to thrust it up my nostril.

'Now. Eat that. And look at the river. You think that has a home? It has no home. It is always moving. But does that mean it is homeless?' Another laugh. 'The water move. I live. You see?'

We ate in silence as we stared at the Thames. Ibrahim gnawed the last string of meat from the leg in his hand, then threw the bone at a passing seagull.

'Birds,' he said. 'Man, this is good chicken.'

13

It started with rain: not the insipid drizzle of an English autumn, but the thick, blasting torrential downpours of a tropical island; rain which smelled of the sea; rain which rose in pitch and violence with each passing second, bouncing and echoing off the pavements and car-roofs in fluctuating and visible sound waves. Those with umbrellas ran, soaked anyway by the water which streaked down their brollies and splashed up from puddles disturbed by their pounding shoes. Those without huddled in doorways, checking the sky, then their wristwatches or smartphones, before succumbing to desperation and stumbling off along the pavements in a weird hopscotch dance.

I was trapped in an archway somewhere on Ludgate Hill, sharing my space with two cyclists and a foreign student. We stared out together through the waterfall which cascaded from the lip of the archway, then looked back at each other to exchange raised eyebrows and exaggerated sighs, but no words. Four teenagers gleefully darted under our shelter, laughing and hooting expletives, wringing their hair out on to each other's shoes and unzipping their jackets to proudly reveal saturated T-shirts. The rest of us moved back to let them in and then exchanged further glances with each other: the kind reserved for those moments when your lift's maximum capacity has been breached.

The teenagers had somewhere to be, and they raced out again, their screams and hollers audible over the rain. Soon, the foreign student took her chances, too, and then finally so did the cyclists, who carefully wended their way out into the traffic and pedalled slowly and deliberately: a calm acceptance of their soaking fate.

It occurred to me that I had nowhere to be and, for once, this was a boon. I could sit here in this cold archway and stay dry, or I could sit in my sleeping bag on the cold Strand and get wet. I slouched down against the wall and opened my knapsack. More for the sake of novelty than hunger, I brewed a Cup-a-Soup on my stove and then drank it with relish as workers and tourists and pensioners took their turns hiding from the rain beneath my archway. They rubbed their hands and wiped their faces and blew their noses, and I hit upon the marvellous business plan of selling hot drinks and renting towels on evenings like this and in spots like this all over London. But I had no water left, the only 'towels' I could offer were my own stinking clothes, and each shelterer never stayed longer than a few minutes. My entrepreneurialism would have to wait for another time.

After an hour beneath the archway, the rain stopped as abruptly as it had started, and I set off back along Fleet Street and the Strand. I was astonished to find my sleeping bag still at my pitch – I had expected to find it washed much further down the road – and even more astonished to see some of my neighbours in their positions, to all appearances asleep, as if the rainstorm had been deflected from their inert bodies by invisible shields.

My sleeping bag was present, but it was uninhabitable. Raising it high and upending it, I watched as a river poured out from its folds and splashed on to the ground before hurrying to join the thin streams and thick puddles which had overrun the pavement.

There would be, I knew, no sleep tonight. No sleep and unimaginable cold. Nothing about me was dry. I slipped into a coffee shop to change clothes in the toilet, but there was no escaping the fact that my one pair of boots, my one sweatshirt and my one coat were all drenched. I tried to evaporate the water from inside my boots with the feeble hand-dryer, but was interrupted by a banging on the toilet door, and fled back out on to the street.

I paced the Strand back and forth, hoping to create some warmth from within, never quite succeeding, grateful only for the fact that, for some reason, I was not tired. My sweatshirt and coat finally began to dry out as I walked – if I watched for long enough, I could see the lighter patches begin to spread across the fabric from my torso outwards – but my boots remained squelching and insufferable. I fancied that, for the tramp, there was perhaps no worse part of the body to remain wet than the feet, and graphic images of wartime trench foot appeared from a realm of my consciousness I could not pinpoint, forcing me into a fast food outlet, where I bought a cup of coffee, took it to the toilets and hit the metal button on the hand-dryer again and again while I sipped the coffee held in one hand and dried my boots held in the other. It was late now, and nobody disturbed me.

Back at my pitch, I placed the bin bag on the pavement, laid my knapsack on top of it, and then sat on that with my back to the wall. My sleeping bag was still too wet to climb into, so I wrapped my coat around me as tight as I could, pulled my hat low and closed my eyes.

I did not sleep that night, but the fleeting drifts of semi-conscious dreams occasionally floated my way, and I was grateful for them. The rain did not return, but the low-hanging clouds remained despite its absence, and beneath them it became the mildest of my nights on London's streets. I was grateful for that, too.

14

It started with rain, and it ended with my flight from the Strand.

By three o'clock in the morning, my right leg had begun to cramp, sending jets of pain up through my body which ripped my dreams apart and opened my eyes. I jumped to my feet, hopping on one leg while I stretched and massaged the other. As the tension dissipated, I tentatively hobbled forward a few steps, then yawned and stretched my arms high above my head. The Strand was quiet, eerie in the ghostly fug of the mist settling from the clouds. I rubbed my eyes and my hands came back wet. Close inspection revealed a thin film of dew on my hat, coat and trousers. There was no wind, no traffic noise, no chatter in the air – just the still and wet serenity of Venice by night.

Without warning, a cry pierced the air. It was stark and shrill, a guttural howl which could have been a cat's territorial war cry were it not for the elongated but clear monosyllable which resounded within it: 'No'.

Another cry, the same, followed, rising out of somewhere from the east, perhaps Fleet Street. Leaving my knapsack on the floor, I went in search of it, skirting the rough sleepers who lay in their puddles. Most remained motionless, though one had lifted his head to locate the source of the noise. Another cry sounded as I passed him, and he turned to look at me, his shock melting into submission as he hurriedly lowered his head and tucked it under the folds of his sleeping bag.

Another cry. This time louder. I was getting closer. In the mist-horizon, I began to define shapes: four on their feet, one on the ground. My approach slowed with stealth as I placed my footsteps close to the wall, encouraged by the obscurity of the mist.

Three men and one woman surrounded a rough sleeper who cowered beneath a blanket on the pavement. The rough sleeper was howling his feral 'No' with increasing frequency and terror while one of the men bent over him, his own voice drowned out by the floored screamer's.

I moved closer. The four were imbued with the false confidence of too much alcohol, the men trendy and well-dressed, the woman in surprisingly little for the climate. The man who bent over the rough sleeper had begun to shout and point an accusatory finger at the sleeping bag.

'... my girlfriend... the fuck... you can't... to my face?...'

'No!' the rough sleeper screamed again. It seemed to be all he could say.

'... had my way... sick fucks like you... castrated, you *cunt*.'

'No!'

The woman began to remonstrate with the two other men. I could dimly ascertain through the mist that both men were smiling while their friend continued with his belligerent outbursts.

'... piece of shit... my taxes... say that to my girlfriend?... kill you, you prick...'

I had not moved for seconds, had frozen against the wall. I needed to get involved, to try and assuage, to alleviate, to make peace, to protect, but my limbs held fast and I could not bring myself to even walk over to the group, let alone announce my presence and attempt rational resolutions. I reminded myself of my appearance and justified my inaction with the thought that another tramp would only serve to raise ire, and that even my voice – which had betrayed me so often on this journey – would carry no wait within their middle-class alcoholic fog, that they would trust only their eyes and not their ears, and that their eyes were already blinded red.

But that was all hokum. I was too terrified to intervene. I was too terrified I might get hurt. It was as simple as that.

As I vacillated, the shouting man stood up straight. The woman began to tug at his arm and the other two men had already started to walk away down Fleet Street. My sense of relief was interrupted in one brutal and swift motion. The man lurched forward with his foot, barely lifting it from the ground nor swinging it behind him, and kicked the rough sleeper so hard in the face that I heard the sickening crunch through the mist. The woman let go of his arm and scarpered off down the street, followed closely by all three men.

My thaw was immediate. I ran to the rough sleeper and dropped to my knees beside him. His hands were pressed tight against his face and small sobs percolated out through his fingers. In the single moment after I asked if he was all right, in the single moment before I found myself sprawled out on my back on the pavement, in the single moment when his hands left his face and one fist punched me hard in the chest – in that single moment, I saw the river of dark blood which coursed down his broken nose, I saw the thick welt already beginning to form around his left eye, I saw the split lip and the strange line across his jaw, and I saw that I recognised him. It was Lom, the deaf man I had met outside Zimbabwe House.

I ran to the nearest phone box (surprisingly difficult to find in Central London), dialled 999, requested an ambulance and then sprinted back to Lom.

But he had already gone. A dry patch of pavement spattered with four droplets of congealing blood was all that remained in his place.

15

Following Lom's example, I decided it was time for me to leave the Strand. I had my bedroom there, and I had even learned how to offset the deleterious effects of a rainstorm (so long as I had the money for a cup of coffee), but my original fears had been confirmed – the Strand was too *open*, and with that came the threat of potential violence which I had seen with my own eyes. To my shame, I realised I had done nothing to stop it happening to another man; what on earth would I do if it happened to me?

I needed somewhere safer: an impossibility, surely, on any of London's streets for the rough sleeper. The threat of violence was part of the package, what you traded in for soup runs, lucrative begging spots and the proximity of other rough sleepers. Never mind that they did not talk to you: it was still better to be among them than to be the only rough sleeper in a place like Hatherleigh.

I packed my sodden sleeping bag into its sheath, shouldered my knapsack and then tucked the bin bag over it so that it could drip-dry while I walked, and I left the Strand at four o'clock in the morning, meandering a circuitous route across London while I searched for a new pitch.

I was heading, I realised at sunrise, back towards Hackney, back towards Dalston. Back towards that couch. There was no other object I coveted more. While the housemates worked, I could sleep; sleep for ten or more blissful hours. Then, when they returned home from work, we could go to the pub, and I could get pissed on two pints.

But something nagged, and it was incessant. In part, it was my pride. The housemates knew where I was going when I left Dalston: to the streets. Returning to the couch would be an admission of failure. They would not be disappointed in me, I knew, but perhaps I would, even though the concepts of pride and rough sleeping were oxymoronic. Yet there was more. Something in me *wanted* to stay on the streets, just for a little while longer, and the nagging came from a means to do it. There was a name somewhere, a name which floated just beyond my reach, and I clawed for it until it popped up and dispelled itself from my lips somewhere in Broadgate.

'Brian Haw.'

I turned on my heel and walked straight to Parliament Square.

Brian Haw might be London's, and perhaps England's, most famous rough sleeper. Or at least he was, for he died just three months before I arrived in London.

On 2 June 2001, the fifty-two-year-old Brian Haw pitched a tent upon the roundabout opposite the Houses of Parliament, and began his political protest against Anglo-American foreign policy regarding Iraq and Afghanistan. Leaving his wife and seven children behind at their home in Redditch, Haw lived in his tent on Parliament Square for the next decade, enduring along the way countless attempted prosecutions by Westminster City Council and a number of short-lived arrests, surviving on the food donations of his numerous supporters. His protest was singular and showed a stamina which many of the Westminster politicians he denounced each day for ten years through his megaphone could not reciprocate. Just five months before his tin anniversary at Parliament Square,

Haw finally left his tent for Berlin, where he was treated for lung cancer. He died five months later, on 18 June 2011, exactly ten years and sixteen days after he erected his tent in Parliament Square.

Despite his death, many of his supporters remained at the protest camp Haw had created. Each of these had their own conclusion regarding Haw's demise.

'You see this traffic? It never lets up. You breathe in these levels of carbon monoxide for ten years, and you try and not get lung cancer.'

'Those bastards over there, in their Houses of so-called Parliament, they did it. I've been here long enough to spot the *agents provocateurs* they send over here looking for information. It was them who poisoned Brian. Not to kill him. Just so they could whisk him away to Germany. And out of here.'

'Brian Haw? Never saw him without a fag in his mouth. Two packets a day easy. I heard he smoked like that since he was fifteen. No surprise.'

Arriving at Parliament Square, I darted across the busy road towards the line of tents. Two quiet men sitting on the kerb ignored me as I approached, as did the Nigerian who hurried back and forth along the pavement, waving his placard and shouting rapid and incomprehensible flurries of vocalisation at the roaring traffic. I came to a gap between two tents. A young and dreadlocked man, dressed in jeans, flip-flops and a football T-shirt, smiled and offered me a Pringle.

'Ian,' he said, pointing at his chest. He wore mirrored sunglasses and I could not tell if he was looking at me, though the angle of his head suggested he was not.

'I'm Charlie,' I said, perching on the kerb next to his folding chair.

'I'm Ian,' he said again. 'I am I an, and inside you, you are, you an. But what are you? *You.* Y-O-U. Why oh you? And why are *you* not letting *me* be what I an?'

'You mean me personally?'

'No, not me. You not as an individual, but you as a concept. You is the opposite of me. You follow?'

'No,' I admitted.

Ian leaned in and turned his face to mine, so that I could see the convex reflection of myself, the confused and unshaven headpiece of a long line of diminishing tents, in his sunglasses. 'It's language, bruv,' he said. 'English is old. Patois is younger. But before English there was Latin, Sanskrit, hieroglyphs, cuneiforms, lines and dots. But, you think, how can we communicate in lines and dots? Yet how do computers communicate? Lines and dots.'

He came to an unexpected stop and removed his glasses. With a blink, his eyes flickered from inquiry to mischief, and he gave a sudden laugh, shaking his dreadlocks and squinting up at Big Ben.

'So what's your story, bruv?' he giggled. It was not just his eyes and tone which had changed, but his whole demeanour, and I wondered if I had just passed some sort of test. Sitting there, he must have had to endure the hectoring of any number of zealots and crackpots, and perhaps the enigmatic speech I had sat through was his way of scaring off others first – if they stayed, they were all right.

I learned later it was not a test. It was classic Ian. Living on Parliament Square, I was to grow close to Ian, and this flitting vacillation between elusive philosophy and warm camaraderie – often interposed by flights of merry or enraged hooliganism – was indicative of his character. As he loved to say of himself: 'Don't mind me, I'm half-mad.' I remembered Orwell's words in *Down and Out*: he had used that very same phrase, 'half-mad', to describe those whom poverty had forced into an eccentric freedom which existed outside of the 'normal' boundaries of behaviour.

I explained to Ian what I was doing.

'Get a tent,' he said immediately. 'Come and live with us for a bit. There's a space next to me. I guess you could call us homeless, but I think we're unique.'

Rising to my feet, I shook his hand and promised I would be back. A few metres away, two old men sat under a Brian Haw banner: they were, they said, 'keeping things going until Barbara is released'.

Barbara Tucker, a friend and contemporary of Brian Haw, had demonstrated alongside him at Parliament Square for a number of years. At the time of my arrival, she was finishing one of her many prison-stints for her refusal to, as one of the men said, 'do what *they* told her'.

'I'd like to come and live here for a bit,' I said. 'Ian's already told me I can pitch up next to him.'

'Who?' one of the men said. I pointed down the tents towards Ian munching on his Pringles, but the man did not follow the direction of my finger.

'Best to leave it for now,' he said. 'We can't recruit just at the moment. But Barbara's out tomorrow. Speak to her. She'll let you know.'

I sat on the kerb beside him and we chatted sporadically. He was in his late sixties or early seventies, wore at least five different layers of clothing and a woolly hat with a wilting bobble which looked like a cat had ripped a chunk from it. His bushy eyebrows were matted with seams of congealed blood. I asked him his name, but he would not tell me. The old man did not sleep on the square, but instead spent every daylight hour sat in his camping chair handing out tiny slips of paper with www.brianhaw.tv scrawled on to them to any passer-by who showed an interest. I was given five.

I asked him if all the tents were occupied, and he admitted that he did not know. There were different groups among them, he explained: his dominion was the four tents formerly inhabited by Brian Haw, Barbara Tucker and their compatriots; the few to the left of them had been set up in order to promote global peace in general; and the rest were 'just the leftovers'.

'Leftovers of what?' I asked.

'See this?' He tapped the metal fencing behind us which skirted Parliament Square's garden. 'This fence is recent. Only last year the whole garden was filled with tents. They called it Democracy Village. But they've all been chased off, and those lot are all that's left of them.' He pointed towards Ian and the tents behind him. 'I don't speak to them.'

CHAPTER EIGHT

LONDON TENT

I

I rushed back to Dalston to beg the use of a tent for a few days. The housemates were keen festival-goers, and I was offered a splendid array to choose from. I settled on a two-man dome, the kind which pops up into a habitable shelter within seconds. It would be ideal for the streets: I did not want to spend an hour on the edge of the road locking together poles and securing groundsheets.

Marcus had made dinner, and I was offered some, along with wine. It was late by the time we finished the meal. Outside, a rainstorm as tumultuous as the previous night's beat against the windowpanes.

'Stay the night,' Marcus implored.

The temptation to do so was irresistible. A large and heavy blanket – bought in some Eastern bazaar; more a rug than a duvet – lay across the couch, a pillow was produced, and the living-room radiator turned up to maximum.

'Here.' Marcus dropped his house keys on to the table. 'Have a lie-in tomorrow. Have a shower. I've got some pasta in the fridge you can have for lunch. Let yourself out whenever you want, lock the door and post the keys back through.'

I followed his instructions to the letter, grateful once again for these kind and wonderful friends of mine.

2

I left the house late in the afternoon the next day, so late that, by the time I arrived in Parliament Square with my knapsack in my hand and the dome tent strapped to my back like a tortoiseshell, it was dark. Nobody was around. The protesters' tents were zipped shut, and the line of other tents seemed shorter than it had the day before. Worst of all, Ian's tent was gone. I wanted to see him again, not just because I had liked him, but because I wanted to prove that I had kept my word and returned. I did not doubt that many had walked along these flagstones over the last ten years, promised to come back and join the fight, and then never been seen again.

From the occasional tent I could hear voices – one laughing, another speaking low and quick, a snorer – but most were quiet, all the doors were closed, and no one sat outside them. Since there were fewer tents than before, there was space at the end of the line next to a small grey bivouac leashed to the fencing with bungee cords. I unzipped my bag, pulled out the tent, undid the clasps, and it popped up on the ground before me, complete and habitable in a second.

A mild wind bounced off the slopes of canvas behind me and, with no inclination to chase my tent out on to the busy road should it be lifted and then carried by the currents, I threw my knapsack into the far end for ballast and tied the guy ropes to the fence.

A beam of torchlight fell on my hands and then travelled up to my face. From within the square's garden, a silhouetted figure appeared and approached me.

'You can't do that,' the figure said.

I was ready for this, had rehearsed my defence for precisely this eventuality. 'Yes I can,' I began. 'I was invited by one of the residents. We all have the right...'

'No, no,' he interrupted. 'I mean you can't pitch your tent at that angle. You're obstructing the entrance.' He pointed at the pavement beneath the far end of my tent. The kerb dipped down to the road, allowing vehicular access to what I could now see was a break in the fencing. 'This is where the construction workers drive in. You're not allowed to get in their way.'

I looked around me. 'So what should I do? Can I pitch on the other side?'

'What is that?' he said, shining his torch on my tent. 'Let me see. Two-man. Not so big. You can turn that around. Vertical. Not horizontal. There's enough room. You won't be in the way, then.'

He was not a large man: of average build and no more. His uniform was pristine and ironed. An epaulette bore the words 'Security Warden'. Aside from the torch, the only other object he carried was a Thermos flask. His hat looked too big for his head, and I wondered if the wind ever carried that away.

'Here,' he said, stepping through the break in the fence and taking hold of one end of my tent. I loosened the guy ropes and he pivoted it around in one thrust. 'That's good.'

'Thanks for your help,' I said. 'But why are you helping me? Shouldn't you be encouraging me to leave? You probably could have convinced me. It's my first time here.'

He laughed. 'You lot are all right,' he said, then walked back behind the fence and into the garden.

Once I had unrolled my sleeping bag and fashioned my coat into a pillow, laid out the belongings I kept in arm's reach at night (bottle of water, matches, penknife, torch), assembled my cooker and made soup in a mess tin – in short, once I had arranged my little home and then eaten dinner in it, I sat outside with a can of lager. The opening of my tent held a little porch, which the security warden had helped me face towards the fence. Here, I had a small enclosure which I could duck in and out of at my leisure.

I mostly stayed within. Those moments where I moved outside to sit with my back against the fence, I found myself flicking my head back and forth up and down the street with each loud noise. Though this was far better than my 'bedroom' on the Strand, I nevertheless felt a vulnerability on this square, camping in the glow of the Houses of Parliament and the acoustics of Big Ben. It was all too open, too noisy, too *famous* to offer that solace which comes when night falls and one locks the windows and doors and shuts the world out.

I kept myself out of sight of the pedestrians who passed on the far side of the road. I wanted no one to see me and, in particular, wanted no one to see me alone. That would only serve to heighten my vulnerability. Inside the tent felt safer, though that rested on an illusion: the illusion that any number of people could be in this tent. That might keep any opportunistic intruders at bay, but the illusion hung on a gossamer thread.

At eleven o'clock, I closed the doorway for the final time and crawled into my sleeping bag. The noise from the passing traffic kept me awake and frazzled. I wondered if it would ever stop, and it did not. In that dark tent, with nothing to focus on but the surging, endless roar of engines, I became acutely aware of how delicate and fragile my shelter was. It rocked and shook in the wake of each passing car, bus and lorry, and headlights seared the canvas with a flashing light show of shadow and silhouette. I began to cultivate a paranoid fantasy. How easy it would be for a car, this late at night, perhaps a drunk driver at its wheel, to momentarily lose its trajectory, climb up on to the kerb and crush us all.

3

I woke in the morning to the spasms which pressed into my bladder. The urge to urinate was indomitable. Opening the tent flap, I saw the impossibility of pissing out from that or anywhere along the street, and instead relieved myself into my water bottle. I could buy another later.

Big Ben chimed eight o'clock, and I left my tent to explore my immediate surroundings in the daylight. The snorer still snored, but the few other voices I had heard the night before were now silent, and any human presence was telescoped down to one man, the old protester I had met two days before, who sat outside the same tent with his fistful of paper. He held a strip out to me as I approached; he did not seem to recognise me.

'Please visit our website. It's important that you do.'

'We met two days ago,' I said. 'I told you I wanted to stay here for a while.'

'That's right,' he nodded, recollection blooming on his gaunt face. It was cleaner than before; the congealed blood in his eyebrows had been washed away, and his stark jawline was freshly shaven.

'Good news?' I hazarded. 'Is Barbara out?'

'Not yet,' he mumbled. 'We're still waiting. Best to leave it for now. We can't recruit at the moment. But Barbara will be out tomorrow and you can speak to her.'

'Actually, I already moved in. That's my tent over there.' I pointed through the fencing at the blue pop-up on the far side.

'Oh, so you're with the homeless lot, are you?' he asked, then swivelled on his chair, and would not speak to me again.

I walked back to my tent, took my sleeping bag from inside it, rolled it into a ball and perched on it out in the open. I studied my environment. My tent sat on the southern aspect of the square, facing St Margaret's Church and, behind that, Westminster Abbey. A panoramic sweep took in the Supreme Court, HM Treasury and Cabinet Office, Big Ben, the Palace of Westminster, and then the abbey again. Ten statues peered over the fencing at me, among them Churchill, Disraeli, Abraham Lincoln, and the youngest, Nelson Mandela. Way above them all, a multitude of cameras peered down at all of us from their rooftop vantage points.

Eleven other tents, all of different colours and proportions, stretched from mine up and around the corner to the eastern aspect of the square facing Big Ben. An invisible demarcation divided them from the two large Brian Haw tents, and then another divided the Brian Haw tents from the 'Peace Box' (a mock old-fashioned Police Box) and the two tents which clustered around it. Even this tiny community had ripped itself into factions: the peace protest (centred around the 'Peace Box'), the anti-war protest (centred around Brian Haw's old tent), and the homeless settlement (centred around nothing). Due to naught but the location of my tent, I was one of the homeless, and was considered accordingly. I did not mind so much.

By midday, still no one had surfaced from my faction's tents. My eyelids hung heavily, but I kept them open with cups of black tea boiled on my miniature stove. One of the security wardens, a different man from the night before, greeted me through the fence.

'You're up early,' he said.

'It's twelve o'clock.'

'That's early for you lot.'

'Do you want a cup of tea?'

'No, thanks.' He pointed to the flask against his hip. It looked identical to the one I had seen fourteen hours before. I wondered if it was part of the uniform.

'Were you here last night?' I asked.

'I do the day-shift. Me and my partner over there. The night guys take over in the evening.'

'I met one of them last night. He was nice.'

'Why wouldn't he be?'

'I don't know. Good question. I suppose I just figured that you lot were here to keep us off the green. I heard there used to be tents there, too.'

He nodded. 'That's part of it. At first, we had a bit of trouble keeping it clear. People jumped the fence at night and tried to sneak in. But that only lasted a few weeks, and it was months ago. No one bothers any more.'

'So why are you still here?'

'Have you ever considered,' he said, fingering the metal body of his flask, 'that we might be here for *your* protection?'

4

With no one around to talk to but the security wardens, I wandered away from Parliament Square. At the foot of the stairs down into Charing Cross Underground, I found a large sign which read: 'It is an offence to lie down in any of these walkways or to deposit anything intended to be used as bedding. The maximum penalty is a fine of up to £500.'

I stood before it, copying the script into my journal, when Justin appeared at my shoulder.

'What are you writing that down for?' His breath was soured with alcohol and his blonde hair hung limply under the weight of grease.

'It might be useful.'

'*It might be useful,*' he imitated. 'Who the fuck are you? That sign's not useful to anybody.'

I placed the journal in my bag.

'I don't like you,' Justin said. 'You got any change?'

I did not like him, either. 'No,' I said.

Justin looked me hard in the eye. He edged his body forward so that his left hand almost touched my right trouser-pocket. *Try it*, I thought. *There's nothing in there.*

'I *know* you,' Justin said. 'Don't I? I've seen you before. I know you.'

'We've never met. I'm sure of it.'

'We've never met, but I've seen you. I've seen you around.'

Perhaps he had. He may have seen me sleeping on the Strand, but it could have been anywhere. For almost two weeks, I had trawled the homeless hotspots in London, and it was not unlikely that our paths had crossed more than once, and that he had recognised me. I had nothing to fear, no cover to be blown: I had lied to no one about my reasons for being on the streets. But his surly, half-drunk aggression left me unnerved. I did not want a confrontation down here in this enclosed space.

'That's it!' he exclaimed, poking me in the chest with his finger. 'You're the little fucker who took out Penthouse, aren't you?'

'Penthouse?' I said. *The magazine?*

'Yeah, you knocked him on his arse at the soup run a few weeks ago. He pissed on your shoes.'

'That wasn't me.'

'Yes it fucking *was*. I know you. You're a little fucking smasher.' The noun seemed ameliorative, and I smiled weakly. 'You got a touch?' he added.

'What?'

'Fuck it. Don't worry about it. I'm just after a touch, is all. What's your name again?'

'Charlie,' I said. 'What's yours?'

'Justin. Sorry about all that, Charlie, but my head's mashed at the moment.'

'No worries,' I said, wondering how to get away from him. I decided to be direct. 'I'm off. See you at the soup run.'

'Where you going?'

I had intended returning to my tent, but I did not want him to know I lived there. Who knew at what hour he might turn up, perhaps with Penthouse, demanding a touch from the little fucking smasher. 'Victoria Street.'

'Hmmm, maybe I seen you there, too. I'll come with you. My pitch is outside Carphone Warehouse.'

'Do you sell *The Big Issue*?'

'Fuck off, do I! Nah, I just get the change.'

We climbed the stairs, circumnavigated Trafalgar Square and walked up Victoria Street together. 'What do you claim?' Justin asked.

'Nothing,' I replied.

'Me neither. The fuckers. Won't give me shit unless I break an arm, get a dog or admit to abuse. But then they've got you right where they want you. Cunts. But I play the system, see. Been on the streets since I was seventeen, so I've never paid a fucking *penny* tax. They hate that. Serves them right. I should be looked after. I'm a human fucking being.'

Two Asian women in prim dress-suits passed us. Justin obstructed their passage and yelled into their faces: 'Spare some change *please*.' The women looked at the ground and skirted around him.

'See that?' he said. 'They're over here, they're rich as fuck, and they won't give me shit. What's going on with this country?'

'They work for their money,' I said, tired of his self-aggrandising. I half-hoped he would hit me so I would have an excuse to leave him.

'Then they're fucking stupid, too. Wasting their lives working. I bet they live in a cushy flat,' he rambled on, 'and I've got to sleep rough every night. Where's the justice in that? We're fucked, you and me, Charlie. Sold down the river by those cunts in government. What the fuck did we ever do to *them*?'

I breathed a sigh of relief as we reached Carphone Warehouse. Justin stopped and sat down, propping his back against its window.

'You can stop here for a bit, if you want,' Justin said.

'No, I've got to go.'

'Where?' His eyes narrowed suspiciously.

I considered my options, only to find my mind blank. 'There's this girl…' I stuttered.

'Ah! Enough said!' he laughed, and then his smile drooped and his voice turned menacing again. 'But if you get a touch, you come see me, yeah?'

5

Back at Parliament Square, I took off my coat and unzipped my tent, ready to dive in and sleep through the rest of the afternoon.

'Charlie!'

The holler hit my ears just as I was stepping into the tent, and I turned around to see Ian running across the road while there was a lull in the traffic.

'You came!' he shouted, running the rest of the way to me, his flip-flops slapping on the concrete. 'I knew you would, man. I told the rest we had a writer coming to stay with us, but they didn't believe me. This your tent?'

The effusive smile on his face and the strength in his arm as he wrapped it about my shoulders made me happy that he was still here.

'This is mine,' I confirmed. 'I pitched up last night. I looked for you, but your tent had gone.'

'Yeah, they took it.' He looked closely at my tent. 'Man, this is exactly like mine. Exactly. Did *you* take it?'

'No!' I said, suddenly guilty beneath the accusation. 'I borrowed this from…'

'I'm just fucking with you!' Ian laughed. 'I know it wasn't you. I saw mine go. I'm over in the Rainbow Tent now.' He pointed at a large, multicoloured dome which faced the Houses of Parliament, a few tents down from Brian Haw's camp. 'They're letting me use it for a bit. It suits me. I'm a sun-baby. You wanna come see?'

We walked over to the Rainbow Tent, where Ian pulled out a tube of Pringles and shared them with me as we sat on the cold pavement. He explained that, just a few hours after we had met and he had invited me to come and live on the square, the police had come for one of their clean-up operations.

'They're fairly regular,' he said. 'Every few weeks, sometimes during the day, sometimes at night, riot vans pile up and take away any unoccupied tents. It's Boris, man. He's a liar. And he's a *bad* liar. He says he respects our right to protest, but he doesn't. He knows he can't evict the people here, but he knows that if no one's in the tent then it can be classed as litter, and he can have it removed. Sneaky, man, sneaky. That's why I stay here as much as I can.'

That day, for the first time in two weeks, Ian had left the square to visit a friend south of the river. When he returned, he found seven of the tents missing. One of them was his, and all the belongings he had kept inside it were gone.

'My *shoes*, man!' he lamented as he told me the story. 'I had such good *shoes* in that tent. And they're *gone*!'

He had, however, arrived home in time to see the dump truck which everything had been thrown into dismount the pavement and drive off around the square. Sprinting after it, he leapt in the back and frantically removed some of his possessions before the truck stopped and he was told to piss off.

'I got some of my clothes and a bit of food, but not my tent. It's a shame, man, that was a good tent. Just like yours. But for some reason they didn't take the Rainbow Tent, even though no one's been in it for the last month. So I'm in that now.'

I felt sorry for Ian, though I could not help but acknowledge a secret gratitude for my own good fortune. If Marcus had not asked me to stay at the house that night – if, as I had planned, I had come straight back to the square – the tent I had borrowed, along with my belongings inside it, may well have been swallowed up by the dump truck. I imagined returning to the Dalston house and trying to explain why, after only a few hours in my care, I had lost their tent. Once again, I found myself inordinately grateful for the seductive lure of that couch.

Ian and I spent the next few hours rationing out the Pringles and talking. He was young, no older than twenty-five, energetic and charming. People often inquisitively strolled along the stretch of tents, usually tourists, and if they were female Ian would fling cheeky one-liners their way, or smile and say: 'I hope your boyfriend tells you how hot you are every day.' Some of the girls marched on, pretending not to have heard, but most smiled bashfully, though none ever gave him their phone number, despite his audacious demands.

'What do I care?' he whispered to me. 'I haven't got a phone.'

While the pedestrians rarely spoke to us, those who passed in their cars did so often. Sometimes people beeped their horns and raised their thumbs over their steering wheels in a gesture of solidarity, but more often than not, drivers shouted imprecations from their open windows, the most common: 'Get a job!'

'Give me one!' was Ian's standard retort.

I told him about the night before when, at three or four in the morning, I had heard the unmistakeable whirr of a bicycle's spokes and a teenage voice call in a sing-song lilt: 'Pikey, pikey, pikey, get a mortgage.'

'That happens,' Ian said. 'You'll notice that, whatever people say, whether it's good or bad, they'll usually say it from the safety of a passing car. They never stop. Whether they're supportive or hateful, they still don't want to come close. They're scared of us, you know.'

'People are generally scared of the homeless.'

'Definitely. And so they dismiss us. You know how I deal with it? I dismiss them back. Fuck 'em. Fuck 'em all.' His voice rose to a shout. 'I'm not one of them! I am me! I *an*!'

Though he was at least six years younger than me, Ian seemed to take the role of my mentor. He carefully explained how to live successfully on the square: detailing the buses which could be hopped for free; the nearby bars and cafes which were either sympathetic or hostile to a rough sleeper who walked in looking for a toilet or a glass of water; the local soup runs and charity outlets which donated food or clothes; and the best places to find discarded cigarette stubs.

'But the jewel is that place,' he said, pointing behind us up Victoria Street to the Methodist Chapel Hall. 'Great toilets in there. I go every day to wash. No one ever says a word. Good people, man.'

He was interested in me and what I was doing – 'This needs to be written. I would do it myself if I had the patience.' – but his longest monologues featured himself and his time at Parliament Square.

'Have I told you about the time I was almost tasered?'

'Definitely not.'

'*Almost* tasered. I was close. I've been getting into trouble with that lot,' he pointed at the policemen who stood outside the gates to the Houses of Parliament, 'since I've been here. They know me. In fact, it was that one right there on the left who almost tasered me. He didn't in the end. But I was stuck in one of those black sheds over there, interrogated for an hour and a half. In my pants.'

'What?' I laughed at the unusual punchline, and Ian laughed with me. 'What did you do?'

'I went on one.' He sighed. Sometimes a look of regret or perhaps self-reproach flashed across his face, as it did then, though it always vanished in seconds. Ian, I suspected, did not do regret. 'Last summer, that whole patch of grass in the middle of the square was filled with tents. "Democracy

Village", we called it. In the centre, we made a little garden for ourselves. For some reason, I don't know why, there was a stone bust of Prince Charles in the garden. So one morning, I was fucking drunk, man, I was just in my pants, and I took the bust into the middle of the road there and sat on it. I sat on Prince Charles's face. The traffic stopped and jammed up. I just stayed there. I'm half-mad usually, but that morning was total. That policeman came into the road and pointed a taser gun at my chest. I'm glad now I heard him and stood up. That's when I ended up in the shed.'

6

I shared my space with three mice: three incautious and intrepid little rodents who became a constant presence in the evenings. I felt sure that, were I to spend enough time living on the square, I would eventually come to refer to them as 'my little friends'. Two were small and fast, and they appeared from the lawn's grass, which rose up over twice their height, by leaping and bounding like insane dogs. The third was fat and bulky, and he shuffled about the porch of my tent in search of food, oblivious to my shoos and waved hands: a tough old London mouse. All three appeared as the sun began to set and then disappeared again when the London night sky's few stars began to twinkle through the light pollution. I never fed them, but this did not discourage them, and in the end I let them scurry about my porch without bother. There was, after all, no one else about to talk to at night on the square.

This was apparently unusual. Ian had explained that afternoon that, the night before I arrived, there had been an altercation between two of the homeless residents. 'It happens every now and then. People get drunk, man. And when they get drunk they fight. I've done it myself.'

His description of the event was sparse. Following a 'tent-party', two of the younger men had got into a fight at four o'clock in the morning. The police had arrived, and everyone was keeping quiet for a few nights.

I pressed Ian for further information. What had they been fighting about? Was it serious? Did the police arrest them?

Ian only responded with the sentence: 'Better you don't know.'

I did not like the undertones of Ian's secrecy. Like Stan, there were clearly some elements of his chosen lifestyle he did not want me to write about.

'You'll get to know some people,' he had said. 'Maybe they'll tell you. We'll all forget about it soon anyway, have another tent-party, and you can find out for yourself. Fuck, man, maybe someone will want to fight *you*!'

With no one about but the mice, I closed up the tent for my second night on the square, strapped my miner's torch to my forehead, and pulled Dickens from my knapsack. But reading, relaxation, was difficult. My mind kept slipping back to that fight, all the withheld information that went with it, and Ian's closing taunt – that someone might want to fight me.

These attempts at immersive involvement in a subject could, I knew, end up backfiring in the face of the writer. When Hunter S. Thompson spent a year living with the Hell's

Angels to gather material for his non-fiction book about them, it all finished when he was 'stomped' by the very men he had befriended. During the year of my first book, when I had travelled about England teaching in its most challenging schools, a thirteen-year-old had launched forward at me to, in his words, 'break your fucking *jaw*', and I had run home to recover for close to a month, unsure if I could continue the journey. He was a teenager, and that punch had, ultimately, never even been thrown. What on earth would I do if a lagered twentysomething rough sleeper took an equal dislike to me and decided it might be fun to see how many kicks it took to make the writer cry?

I shuddered at the thought, a thought which, in that dark and loud tent, morphed into my second paranoid fantasy: of someone – anyone – upending a jerrycan of petrol over my tent and striking a match to the hyperflammable material while I slept inside. Those football hooligans I could hear marching past with their tone-deaf, drunken chants, they weren't the kind of folk you wanted outside your tent in the middle of the night, your unwanted tent in the middle of a city, of the *capital* city, no less! They could do it. And, if not them, maybe someone who lived here, one of my supposed comrades. If they fought each other anyway, why not pick on the new guy with his journal and his posh accent? It was a fantasy which I could not dispel as I lived on the square; a fantasy which grew exponentially when I encountered Greg.

7

It came as some surprise to me when I checked my watch and discovered it was eight o'clock in the morning. That meant I had slept for a full six hours. It was hardly refreshing, but I nevertheless felt the tiny achievement, and decided to celebrate with a wash at the Methodist Chapel Hall.

A spattering of well-dressed men and women gathered about the doorway and foyer, but none paid me any heed as I passed them and made directly for the toilets. The cold water was a balm for my skin, which stretched and prickled along my arms, and I gasped with exhilaration each time I plunged my face into the full sink.

The campsite was quiet again when I returned, but later that day a few of the homeless began to emerge from their tents. The first was Marek, a Polish man who spoke with a hesitation born from a lack of confidence rather than a lack of vocabulary. Our conversation was slow and methodical, but meaning always prevailed in the end.

Marek had moved to England at the start of the year. He knew no one in London, but used his meagre savings to secure a room in shared accommodation and used his abilities as a skilled labourer to gain employment on a construction site. He had become friendly with the four other Eastern Europeans, none of them Polish, in his flat, bonding over a mutual love of smoking weed. They could not afford to frequent the bars or clubs at night, and so instead loaded up on bong-hits at the flat and then drove around the city late at night: in search of what, Marek could not explain. The owner of the car was the only one of the group to hold a licence, but he gladly let the others drive whenever he fancied a spliff-break in the back seat.

One evening, one of the unlicensed drivers, stoned beyond belief, misjudged his breaking distance, swerved wildly to avoid a cyclist, and rolled the car. Marek woke up in hospital, his right leg mangled. He showed me the long, twisting scars down his thigh and behind his knee.

'With this,' he said, 'no work. So no money. So no flat.'

He had spent two weeks in the hospital, and when he left he found his friends had all returned home, his belongings were nowhere to be seen, and the flat was already occupied by five others.

'Why didn't you go home, as well?'

'I cannot.'

'Do you need money?'

'No.' He pulled a Polish chequebook from his pocket, thumbed through it like a flick-book, and then produced a cheque guarantee card from the same pocket. 'My money is here. But look. Not cash card. And no one will take my cheque. Do you know any money shops to cash my cheque?'

I did not.

'But there is money here! I sell you?'

'No,' I said.

With no money, no work and no accommodation, Marek had slept rough on the Strand for a week before meeting Ian on the square, who pointed him towards one of the unoccupied tents and told him it was his if he wanted it. Marek had been there for the last fifteen days. He remarked elusively on someone who told him he was eligible for benefits and a crisis loan, and that he was waiting for them to arrive so that he could move out of the tent and into a flat, but when he talked he gave the clear impression that he knew they would never come, and that he was stuck in this alien city living in a tent beneath a massive clock.

Movement caught my eye. It was Ian, appearing from the doorway of the Rainbow Tent and stretching luxuriously. He strolled across the flagstones and greeted Marek and me with a wide grin.

'Ian,' Marek said. 'Do you know a money shop where I can cash a cheque?' He held the chequebook out, and Ian took it from his hand.

'Yeah, I can help you out with this, man,' Ian said, putting his arm around Marek. 'I'll take you to a place in the morning. Just make the cheque out in my name.' He laughed, winked at me, and Marek slid the chequebook back into his pocket. 'Either of you got any food? I'm starving.'

'Come over to my tent and I'll cook something up for us,' I said.

'*Cook?*' Ian exclaimed.

We walked down the strip to my tent and I unzipped the door. Ian jumped inside and stretched his arms out to touch both walls. 'Man, this is *exactly* like my tent. You sure it's not?'

I pulled the camping stove, the mess tins, two cans of beans and half a loaf of bread from my knapsack.

'Fuck me,' Ian whistled. 'Look at that. What else you got in here?' He grabbed my bag and stuck his hand in, rummaging through my clothes. 'Money?'

'No.'

'Shit. I was thinking of robbing you.'

'You could try. But it'd be pointless.'

Ian laughed, nudged me with his shoulder, and bounded out of the tent. 'Come on then, Chef. Make us a fucking feast.'

I cooked the beans in one tin and set it on the ground with the bag of bread next to it. We took turns folding our slices and dipping them into the beans. As soon as we finished, Marek produced a bottle of water from his pocket, washed out the tin, and handed it back to me. Ian lit a joint and leaned back against the fence.

'I could do with one of those,' he said, nodding at the stove. 'Maybe I will rob you. You owe me for the tent.'

The cheeky glint in his eye seemed to diminish, though perhaps that was the weed. A man and woman walked past and peered over at us behind the tent.

'Diana! Greg!' Ian shouted. 'Check this fucker out! He just *cooked*!'

Diana and Greg sat next to us. Ian beamed happily, but I noticed that Marek had edged out of the circle slightly. He looked uncomfortable. Ian made the necessary introductions.

'Have you got any mixed herbs?' Diana asked inexplicably.

'Err, no,' I faltered. 'I mostly live on a diet of beans and soup.'

'Ho!' Greg said. 'It speaks English!' Then he opened his copy of the *Metro* newspaper, and did not talk to me again for the rest of the day.

Offsetting Greg's belligerence, Diana embodied kindness and felicity. She talked and she laughed and then she talked again, always with enthusiasm regardless of the subject, and never stopping for breath. Her few questions were succeeded by a pause, and then she would navigate whatever the answer was back to herself, and happily espouse her thoughts on the subject from her own personal point of view. Her accent was round and Mancunian, and, while she started a topic loud and full of confidence, her voice quickly dropped in pitch so that one had to move closer to her to hear her words – a tactic I wondered if she induced on purpose. Diana liked nothing more than to host an intimate one-on-one lecture.

Happy to listen, I became her captive audience for the next few hours while Ian smoked, Greg read his paper, and Marek stood up to limp back to his tent. Diana had been homeless for two years and had lived on the square for the best part of them. She was in her early forties, perhaps, and shared the largest of the tents with Greg, though it was never clear whether they were an item. She took to me almost maternally and, perhaps disappointed that Greg seemed determined to ignore me, she tried to draw him into our conversation.

'Greg, Charlie's writing a book. Isn't that good?'

Greg grumbled something incoherent and continued with his paper.

'I write, too,' she said. 'I want to write something about my daughter. I know a publisher who's interested. I'll tell him about you.'

Diana's way of linguistic diminuendo meant that I could only follow each of her sentiments halfway through until her voice became a low and inaudible mumble. She had children, but I did not catch how many; she loved them, but I did not catch how much; she wanted them back, but I did not catch how she was going to do it. Something had happened two years ago, something big, but it remained an enigma until much later. I gathered it was that which had put her on the streets, that which had wrested her from her family. There was a court case pending, which she often referred to possessively, though she never explained her role within it, nor what it was intended to achieve. Any questions I threw her way were considered and then discarded for a more favourable tangent.

'I'm going to get my daughter back, and then my son, but I need to get through my court case first…'

'When I get a place, I can take that to my court case and then…'

'That's all come up at my court case, and if I can just show them that…'

There was a hint of Kafka in our dialogue. All communication rattled around the edges and then spiralled towards her court case, but whatever her court case was remained a dark and unfathomable hole which swallowed definitions and then spat us back up to start all over again, encased in intrigue but never satisfied.

Somehow, we got on to the subject of mice. Diana wanted to show me the destruction they had wrought on the inside of her tent, and so the four of us stood and walked up the line. As we reached her tent, three men walked past us.

'Greetings!' Ian said. 'Welcome to Democracy Village!'

While his fellows walked on, the largest of the three stopped, looked at Ian, offered him a weird smile, and then followed his friends.

'What the fuck was that all about?' Ian said, staring after them.

'He squared up to you, mate,' Greg told him. 'Prick.'

'Look at this!' Diana called from the opening of her tent. 'Those mice!'

'In a minute, in a minute,' Ian said, still looking at the three men, who seemed to be inspecting each tent they passed with careful scrutiny. 'What're they doing? Let's see if they come back this way.'

'Cops, mate,' Greg said. He looked briefly at me. 'Checking us out. Pricks.'

We watched as the three came to the end of the row and walked a slow lap around the last tent: mine.

'If those fuckers go in your tent,' Ian said, 'we'll do 'em.'

Looking satisfied, the three men left my tent and began the walk back up the southern aspect of the square towards us.

'Cops,' Greg mumbled. 'Sure of it.'

Ian walked forward and stopped directly before the man who had smiled at him. 'Why you looking at me like you know me?' Ian shouted into his face. His whole demeanour had changed, from the gleeful 'sun-baby' to an angry and confrontational yob. The man smiled back at him.

'Why you looking at me like you know me?' Ian repeated.

'Leave it, Ian,' Diana called.

I looked over at Greg, who was also smiling.

'Come on,' Ian shouted. 'Why you looking at me like you know me?'

The other two walked on, and Ian's opponent, always smiling, back-stepped away from his antagonist.

'*Why you looking at me like you know me?*' Ian shouted as the three rounded the corner and moved on to the Peace Box.

'Fucking cocksucker,' Ian breathed heavily. 'You see the way he was looking at me?'

Greg walked into Diana's tent and, without a word, zipped up the doorway behind him while Diana was still inside. Ian, disconcerted, one leg twitching, turned to me.

'Thanks for the beans, Charlie,' he said, and then marched off back to the Rainbow Tent, where he stood and stared at the three men until they crossed the road and disappeared over Westminster Bridge.

8

If I ever made friends on Parliament Square, it was with Ian, Diana, Marek and, to some extent, Greg. For the rest of my time there, we became a group, a social circle, and, though Greg never really accepted me, I think the rest did, and when we spent time outside our tents, we spent it together. Others would pass by, nod, swap sentences or poke their heads from their tents and tell us to shut the fuck up because they were sleeping, but our pack was five-strong, and it remained as such until I left.

There were, however, two others I met on Parliament Square: two others who were not so much a part of our group but who I still spent a meaningful amount of time with, though I would not come to know their full stories – the information they kept hidden from us all – until after I left.

Their names were Rolly and Rudy, a young couple who looked to be on the verge of their twenties. I met them only during the evenings, for they begged full-time during the days, always on separate pitches since, as Rolly explained to me, the 'punters' did not give money to couples. 'If they see you've got someone, they think you must be doing all right.'

I was often amazed by how much they pooled each day, more so by their cavalier way of flashing it about the campsite at night. Once, Rudy held up a twenty-pound note an old lady had given her that day, and I did not like the way Greg looked at her. I remembered Ian's teasing threat of robbing me, and wondered if this lot ever stole from each other. It was not improbable.

The first night I met Rolly and Rudy, they had had a very good day, begging close to eighty pounds between them. They celebrated with a crate of lager and generously shared it out amongst the seven of us. Rolly wore an old leather jacket with 'Peace to all Jews' spray-painted in yellow across the back, and his flabby paunch suggested diabetes. Rudy found it hard to sit still. In fact, she often did not sit at all, but crouched low to the ground, her knees bouncing with nervous energy. She spoke in a street patois which seemed too conscious to be genuine, and when I looked at her closely I realised she was younger than I had at first imagined. The two of them would have been called 'crusties' fifteen years ago, when Swampy made the front page for inhabiting a tree in protest against the Newbury Bypass, when The Levellers headlined festivals, and when a white person with dreadlocks was either a hippy, a backpacker or an eco-warrior, or possibly all three.

It was perhaps this thought, coupled with the cans of lager, which led me on to describe a protest I had once attended in the mid-1990s against the construction of a bypass in Cornwall. Rudy listened with barely concealed disinterest.

'But when me and my friend turned up, there was no one else there. Just us two with our placards in the middle of a hundred workmen who laughed and told us to fuck off before they got nasty.'

'It's the system, man, innit,' Rudy said. 'You gotta fight it *true*. Dey wan' us all as, like, their slaves, y'get me?'

'Do you go on many protests here?'

'Nah, bruv, I doan protest. Not even protesting *here*. Make no. Life is good, right? I got no issues.'

That was clear enough. Both Rudy and her boyfriend were euphoric in their homelessness and their love for each other. Young and happy, with time to waste and the romantic angst of the teenager, they seemed to treat their life on the streets as a game. If it was, it was a game with stark undertones which I wondered how they managed to ignore.

Rolly was pointing to the welts and cuts on his forehead where his skin was broken. He said they had come from the baton of a policeman, and he described the beating with pride. 'That was the first hit,' he pointed at a fresh scab over his left eyebrow. 'I was still standing after, so that was the second.'

'Fucking cunts,' Ian growled, increasingly fidgety and angry as he drained the beers.

'Laughed in his face, dintcha?' Rudy prompted.

'Laughed, and then *spat* in his face,' Rolly replied. 'That's when I got this one.'

'You shouldn't have done that,' Diana said.

'Why the fuck not?' Ian shouted. 'Give the fuckers back some! Who gives them the right to piss all over us all the time?'

'Fell after that one,' Rolly continued. 'Smacked my head here.'

'Then they kicked you, right?' Greg muttered.

'Couple of boots in the ribs. Nothing I couldn't handle. I just laughed again and shouted "peace be with you".'

'Peace be with you!' Rudy imitated.

I looked over at Marek, who had understood perhaps half of the conversation, and seemed horrified with it. A whirl of questions spun about my mind. Why had the police officers beaten him? What had Rolly done? Why hadn't they arrested him? And, most importantly, why was no one else asking these things? Ian, Greg and Diana seemed to follow the dialogue as if it was commonplace, but could it really be?

'Why did they do it?' I finally asked.

Rolly gave me a blank look while Rudy sniggered.

'Shut up, Charlie,' Greg said.

9

Greg began to trouble me. There was a grudging amicability to his actions – when he offered around his joints, water or the bags of mixed nuts he fed from incessantly, he always included me; when he returned to the square each morning with a copy of the *Metro* and each evening with a copy of the *London Evening Standard*, he became used to passing them directly on to me once he had finished his slow and methodical perusal – but a manifest antagonism lay buried in each word he exchanged with me.

It was not long before he revealed why. 'You sound like you were born with a *massive* plum in your mouth.'

'I'm from a working-class background. I'm just well educated. There's a difference,' I said.

'Yeah, he's self-educated,' Diana chimed in, though I didn't know how she had arrived at that conclusion, for I was not.

'Still,' Greg mumbled. 'Not one of us.'

I had never claimed to be; indeed, I had come clean to each of them about my reasons for being there the first time I met them.

Diana had noticed Greg's reticence around me and had told me a little about him. In his forties, he had been on the streets since he was a teenager. For the last six years, he had lived in Victoria Square with a changing group of others, none of whom he had ever grown to like or trust.

'He doesn't really like any of us, either,' Diana explained. 'He doesn't like or trust anyone. He wouldn't speak to Ian for the first week. Thought he was too obvious.'

Diana had met Greg one night in Victoria Square and had invited him to Parliament Square, where he had moved into her tent and then lived there with her for the past month. As always, much was left unsaid, and I was never sure of their relationship status, nor if he even liked or trusted her.

'You could be police,' Greg said to me once. 'You could be a journalist. If me and my mates was to hang around with you, if you properly lived with us for a year, say, and then one day you disappeared, and someone said to me, "You know that Charlie? He was undercover", I would believe it.'

'Surely if I was undercover I would have fed you some story about being homeless myself?' I remembered the Cornish coast, where I had toyed with the idea of concocting a back-story but had dismissed it instantly. 'The last thing I would say is that I'm a writer.'

'I know, man,' Greg said. 'That's the only reason I'm talking to you now.'

From then on, Greg liked to call me 'Undercover'.

'You want some nuts, Undercover?'

'Undercover, you get fifteen down on the crossword?'

'Do you puff, Undercover?' he asked, toking on the stub of a joint.

'No,' I said.

'See. That just makes you more suspicious.'

He laid the roach on to the rim of his beer can, took a pretend swig, and then passed the can to Ian, who took it, removed the joint, cupped it in his palm, took a draft of beer, and passed the can back. I thought of these clandestine motions, of Greg's refusal to sit on the aspect of the square facing the Houses of Parliament and the ever-present guards at the gate, of his wordless departures when police vans slowed beside us during their routine circumambulations of the square, and concluded that it was unjustifiable to call me the suspicious one.

10

Time passed on the square rapidly: a surprise when the ringing machinations of Big Ben punctuated every hour. I soon spent all the money I had taken out in Portishead and ripped open my jacket to get at my emergency hundred pounds.

Unlike Rolly and Rudy, I kept it hidden, but it diminished nonetheless, mostly on beer, for I was drinking every day. It was common to begin in the afternoon, something to do while we sat with our backs against the fence and talked about nothing. Soon, I found myself to be the regular. While Diana or Greg or Ian or even Marek disappeared for a day or a night, I remained on the square, leaving only to wash and defecate at the Methodist Chapel Hall. With time, my brain muted the traffic and my skin snubbed the cold. This was far easier than I had ever imagined; was even, in a perverse way, appealing. I had no work to go to, no bills to pay, and no expectations to disappoint myself with. When I woke, later and later each morning, my initial thought was of when I should take my first beer. If I smelled rotten, I was unaware of it.

Ian had been gone for two days. He returned to find me sitting with Marek, who was teaching me Polish words. 'I think you like it here, Charlie,' he said.

I squinted up at him, high on the short boost my current can of lager had afforded. 'Where you been?'

'Got a girl,' Ian said, winking at me. 'She is hot, bruv. *Hot*. Been staying at hers for the weekend, but she had to go to work today. I let myself out.'

Work, I thought. *Is it Monday?*

Ian dropped a plastic carrier bag between me and Marek. Inside it were branded cans of ready-mixed rum and cokes, gin and tonics, whisky and lemonades.

'Booty!' Ian shouted, sitting down and cracking open a gin and tonic. 'Let's get fucking drunk!'

'You want anything, Marek?' I asked, rising to my feet.

He rummaged in his pocket, producing a few pound coins. 'Cider.'

I took the cash and walked up the road to the Victoria Street Sainsbury's. I knew that, while we shared company, stories and sometimes food, we did not share alcohol on the square. Rolly and Rudy were the only ones who had ever willingly handed a drink to someone else, and I had not seen them for some time. At the supermarket, I bought a two-litre plastic bottle of cider for Marek and an eight-pack of on-offer lager for me. When I returned, Diana and Greg had appeared from their tent and were filling their plastic cups from a bottle of white wine. Ian rose to his feet as I sat, for behind me a pretty woman was nosing about our tents and taking photographs.

'You look *good*,' Ian called as she passed. 'You know that?'

'I have an idea,' she smiled as she walked on beyond us.

'Don't be such a tart, Ian,' Diana said, grabbing his coatsleeve and pulling him back into the circle. 'You've got a girlfriend.'

'Man can have more than one girlfriend, you know?'

'Did you hear what she said?' Greg grinned. 'I have an idea. An *idea*. Mark that word.'

'She's got an *idea*, bruv.'

'She's got an idea, all right.'

Greg rose to his feet and playfully punched Ian on the arm. Ian, laughing, punched him back.

'That's really nice,' Diana said quietly to me. 'Greg's got a chip. You know that. He puts up walls. But underneath it is the kindest person ever.' She smiled as she looked at the two who had twenty years between them. Greg had grabbed Ian in a headlock and was pretending to swipe his can while Ian beamed and giggled. 'They're bonding,' Diana said, and her smile then was maternal, and quite beautiful with it.

That afternoon was giddy and flushed with an abundance of drink for everyone. While Ian and Greg continued to bond, Marek drank contentedly from his large bottle, and Diana turned to me.

'It's nice when it's like this,' she said. 'I've been homeless a while, but this is my favourite place. People get on here.'

'There was a fight the night before I arrived.'

'Don't pay any attention to that. It doesn't happen much.'

'Ian said it happens all the time.'

Diana looked over at Ian, who was rolling a joint while Greg stood in front of him and blocked him from view of the traffic. 'You shouldn't believe everything Ian says. He's a lovely boy, but he drinks too much, and it makes him wild. You seem to drink a lot, too.'

'I'm just trying to fit in,' I lied. 'We all drink too much here. *You* drink too much.'

'No, I don't,' Diana said, picking up the bottle of wine. 'I'll have half of this, and I won't have any more. I'll go to bed. Greg can have the rest.'

Diana did drink her half, but when Greg swallowed his last cup he produced another bottle from the tent, and Diana gladly let him fill her glass. I had already noticed that Greg and Marek could drink and smoke for twelve hours without any noticeable effect, while Diana and Ian grew inebriated after just a few. The latter was already sprinting widths across the three-lane road before us, weaving in between the slow-moving rush-hour traffic while Greg cheered him on from the pavement. Diana, on the other hand, had become maudlin and solipsistic.

'I don't think people understand what it's like for us here... they all think it's an easy way out, but it's not... it's not easy at all... I wouldn't be here if I didn't have to be... I'd be back in Brazil... I lived there for two years... always said I'd return... but I've got my court case, and there's nothing I can do... when I get my daughter back, she'd like you, when I get her back... she wants to go to Brazil, but he won't let her... if we could live out there together, now, that would be easy... but not this... but no one knows that... they shout at us and make jokes... what do they know?... that's why what you're doing is good... I write a lot, too... hey, Greg!'

Greg turned from his earnest conversation with Ian, who rocked back and forth on his heels, impatient at the interruption. 'What?'

'You should take Charlie to Victoria Square. Introduce him to some people there.'

Greg laughed without mirth. 'Nah, I ain't doing that.'

'Why not?' she remonstrated.

'I just ain't.'

'Why not? It'd be good for his book.'

Greg looked at her. 'You think I'm gonna go down there and tell them there's a writer wants to speak to them?' He laughed again, and then turned his attention to me. 'You go down there,' he said, 'and they won't talk to you. They won't tell you anything. They'll just try and get you pissed and stoned. And then...'

'But he needs material for his book,' Diana continued.

'It's all right,' I interrupted. 'I don't need it.'

'Got enough from us, have you?' Greg said, sitting down next to me. There was a look in his eyes, a quiver in his lips, which I did not like. 'Let me ask you this, Undercover,' he said, 'you're writing a book about tramps, right?'

'Yes,' I replied. I felt the lager begin to churn uneasily in my stomach, and noticed that Ian was no longer staring at the traffic, but was instead staring at me with an expression I could not decipher.

'All right,' Greg said. 'All right, Undercover. So tell me this. How do *you* define a tramp?'

I considered the question. There was an edge to it, and I knew that a thoughtless response could cost me. 'I think a tramp is someone who has purposefully taken to the road.'

Greg nodded in approval. 'That's good,' he said. 'Yeah. But you *do* know, don't you, that writing your book, you're gonna meet people, people you might not want to know. People who can take you down into...' He paused, searching for the right expression, finally settling on an unnerving cliché. '... a den of iniquity.'

Ian was still watching me. Marek had opened his eyes. Diana had turned her head to face the traffic. I felt suddenly sick, and perhaps it showed, for Greg laughed.

'I don't mean anyone's gonna *kill* you, bruv,' he said. 'Not physically.'

What the fuck did that mean?

'But it's you, mate. *You*. Your whole demeanour. Your *voice*. You're obviously not one of us. And people will react to that. You know?'

Greg was no longer sitting. His knees had pushed him up into an awkward crouch which tilted him heavily towards

242

me. His right hand was in his jacket pocket; his left reached out and picked up the empty wine bottle. It slipped unsteadily in his loose grip. 'You know?' he repeated.

Ian's voice broke like a wave over us. 'Fuck… *this*!' he shouted, and ran down along the line of tents to the western aspect of the square. Greg dropped the bottle, which clanged with a jarring resonance on the flagstones, and rose to his feet. Diana and Marek were quick to follow. I remained seated, frozen to my spot.

'Ian, what the fuck?' Greg shouted.

'Ian, get down from there!' Diana called.

Marek laughed.

I turned around to see Ian scaling the statue of Robert Peel. As he reached the figure's platform, he sat astride it, wrapping one arm around one of the statue's legs and gesturing with his other arm for one of us to throw up his can of rum and coke. We clustered around the monument's base as he hung from Peel's leg and called to the universe: 'What's underneath when you peel back the black from the black man?'

The two security wardens approached and called for Ian to come down. He ignored them. Perhaps satisfied that they had done their duty, they then produced mobile phones from their pockets and took pictures of him.

'What happens?' Ian continued to shout. 'What happens when you peel back the black from a black man? What's underneath? What happens?'

Then the police arrived.

II

We scattered like cats. Greg disappeared first, followed by Diana and Marek. Ian nimbly vaulted down from the statue and walked the long way around the square to the Rainbow Tent. I had the shortest distance to cross, but as I unzipped my tent I looked up to see that everybody else was already inside their own.

The police van drove once around the square and then came to a rest beside my tent. I sat in the porch, making a pretence of tying my shoelaces. Two officers appeared at the opening. They did not bend down.

'All right, mate?' came a voice from somewhere above their knees.

I lurched out and rose to my feet, careful not to stand too close to the two officers for fear that my breath reeked of alcohol.

'All right?' the policeman repeated, looking me up and down with a casual half-smirk.

'Good evening, officer,' I replied. 'Is there a problem? Can I rectify it?' If, as Greg suggested, I really did have a plum in my mouth, it seemed to ooze politesse and verbosity whenever directed at the police. I regaled myself with the conclusion that I liked to confuse them, that the last thing they would expect to hear from this street-dwelling tramp was articulate eloquence. But I wonder now, in hindsight, if it was born of some fundamental shame, a kind of code for: *Don't arrest me, I'm not one of them.*

'You can't stay here,' he said.

'May I ask why? I've spent myriad days here already, and I've caused no harm nor trouble.' If such ridiculous language came from shame, the shame is all mine now as I report it.

'See this?' The policeman gestured at the section of fence between my tent and the lawn. 'This is the entrance for the construction workers. We need to keep it clear so they can drive in.'

'I've had this conversation with the security wardens.' I noticed the mute officer roll his eyes at that appellation. 'They even helped me move my tent around so I wouldn't be causing an obstruction. So far, I've obstructed nobody.'

'Have any workers driven in while you've been here?'

'No, but I'm well away from the entrance. I can't see how my tent could possibly cause a problem.'

'Well, it *is* causing a problem, isn't it? I've just told you.'

I considered my options. I could argue centimetres and inches, but I could tell from the staunch expression on this policeman's face that he had picked his fight, and that no matter what I said I would lose. He had decided to move me on.

'I'll put my tent over there,' I said, gesturing to a spot next to Marek's tent which had been freed up two nights before.

'No can do. You've got to move.'

'But I've got nowhere else to go,' I lied. 'If I pack up now, I'm just going to end up sleeping rough on the Strand.'

'Sorry, mate. It's the law.'

'No,' I said, 'no, it's not. The law says we have a right to protest here. The House of Lords passed it.'

'The law says that *they* can protest here,' he replied, pointing over at the Peace Box and the Brian Haw tents. 'What exactly are *you* protesting against?'

I changed tack. 'I've been to St Mungo's in Camden. I've been to the Homeless Unit at the Charing Cross police station.' The name-drops had no discernible effect. 'At the latter in particular, I was told that the primary purpose of Westminster's police force regarding homelessness is to reduce the number of rough sleepers each night. I asked if this place, Democracy Village, counted as rough sleeping. I was told that, technically, it didn't. Technically, the people here have shelter. Technically, we're not rough sleeping. Aren't I doing you a favour by sleeping here and not on the street?'

The policeman laughed, though not without friendliness. 'No,' he said. 'No, you're not doing me a favour.'

'Look,' I remonstrated. 'It's half seven. It's getting dark. No construction workers are coming here tonight, are they? Just let me spend the night here, and I promise I'll be gone in the morning.'

The policeman turned to his colleague and uttered something inaudible. He turned back to me. 'I'm due back here tomorrow afternoon. Two, three o'clock. If you're still here, I'll arrest you.'

I was prepared to go only so far with my tramping, and my remit did not include arrest. At seven o'clock the next morning, I packed up my things and left, leaving a note and a few cans of lager outside the Rainbow Tent for Ian. Above the beginnings of the Central London morning rush-hour traffic, I could hear him snoring inside.

12

I had slept well that night for, within an hour of the police's departure from Parliament Square, I had decided on my next and final sleeping-spot. Thanks to those morning *Metro*s and late-afternoon *London Evening Standard*s passed on to me with unwavering regularity by Greg, I had for some time, and with some interest, been reading about another impromptu city campsite which had planted itself outside St Paul's Cathedral and then grown exponentially each day. It was, from what I read, for I had not personally visited it, a fundamentally political protest, with no homeless contingent as flaunted at Parliament Square, and though this did not interest me as such, I was not yet ready to go home, and this was still, to some extent, another way of living on the streets.

The Occupy London movement began in October 2011, as a gesture of solidarity to the Occupy Wall Street protest in New York and a number of other offshoots in capital cities across the world. A non-violent protest and demonstration against a number of issues – among them, social injustice, economic inequality, the rise of unemployment and the decline of affordable housing – the original intent of the occupiers was to build an encampment in Paternoster Square outside the London Stock Exchange. Getting wind of the planned demonstration, perhaps from the Facebook campaign which started it, the police got there first and sealed off the entrances to Paternoster Square, citing its private-property status as their lawful reasoning. Spreading out from the barred entrance, the protesters – some three thousand of them – gathered outside the adjacent St Paul's Cathedral. Searching for an alternative, they realised it was right beneath their feet – *public* land – and a hundred tents were pitched outside the cathedral within an hour, where they remained for the next four months.

I arrived in the first of those four months, and already over two hundred tents sat in neat blocks and lines across the square and down around the side of the cathedral, demarcatory avenues snaking between them to create a surprising orderliness amongst the proliferation. 'Welcome to Tent City!' an occupier called out to me, patting the pop-up on my back and then disappearing into the crowds before I could ask him where to pitch.

It was all a far cry from my last spot, closer perhaps to the Glastonbury Festival than the Parliament Square protest, filled with large marquees advertising live music and DJ sets on propped-up chalkboards, one tent even housing an upright piano with a young girl tapping out a lurching Chopin number across its keys; impromptu games of football and other irreverent alternatives where the ball was bounced heavily against the walls of the cathedral; short theatre performances; synchronised dances; face-painting; a cinema; four Portaloos (always 'Out of Order'); a first-aid tent; an information and reception zone; free tea and coffee; free meals from the large canteen; and a meditation tent lit by hanging bulbs which were powered by free-standing solar panels.

Many of those who strolled amongst the tents were curious tourists, but the supporters were conspicuous with their badges and warm clothing, their flyers and, sometimes, masks. Some were foreign, some were older 'lefties', some were ageless and dreadlocked, but most were young men without jobs. It soon became easy to spot who stayed overnight and who did not: the day-supporters were often determined and angry; but the real occupiers who slept in their uncomfortable tents each night spent their days in camping chairs supping from styrofoam cups of coffee and discussing anything that came to mind. 'Do you want me to teach you English?' came a voice from the tents as I passed. These people seemed to have all the time in the world.

Spaces became discernible amongst the clusters of tents as I sauntered up and down the makeshift alleyways. Former occupiers had evidently left these perfectly sized pitches and not returned, though others were already arriving. Three men were building an old-fashioned tent out of rusty poles and moth-eaten canvas on the brink of a rectangular settlement.

'Who do I speak to about pitching up?' I asked.

'What do you think this is, a campsite?' one wheezed as the wind caught his section of canvas and ripped his arms skyward.

I looked around at the two hundred tents and resisted the urge to sarcasm. 'Yes,' I said.

'Pitch wherever you fucking well want.'

Wherever I wanted seemed discordant. This clearly *was* a campsite, an ordered one at that, and I had no inclination of lying down where I would only be in the way. I noticed the large and battered tent of my interlocutor was beginning to protrude out on to the walkway beyond the invisible line against which all its neighbours had been pitched.

'You didn't ask anyone, then?' I said. 'You just set up?'

'Who am I going to ask? The *Dean*?'

'I'm looking forward to living near you,' I replied.

He scowled at me and then set his attention back to the tent, which had inflated like a hot-air balloon and looked ready to carry all three of them off into the torrid London air.

That evening, those three men were asked to take down their tent and move over to the Finsbury Park site since they were obstructing the public walkway. They had not understood the unwritten regulations of this place, but I had – this demonstration was perceptibly British, from its structured disposition to its neat classifiability to its determination that it would take place over the most inclement months of the North Atlantic calendar. I had no inclination to step on any toes, no wish to ignore the simple needs for space and order in this place which, though novel and unprecedented, was peopled by those with an innate loathing of chaos.

I asked four separate people where I could pitch my tent, but none knew. The last referred me to the information and reception zone, but no one there could tell me, either. I decided to try one last time. He seemed a likely candidate, stepping from his own tent and then walking up and down before the cathedral bearing a placard which read: THIS IS NOT A PROTEST. THIS IS A RIGHT.

I stopped him with a hand on his shoulder. 'Excuse me,' I said. 'Do you know whereabouts I could pitch?'

He looked at me as if he was Jesus. 'It would not be my place to tell you where you can go.'

The answer took me by surprise. 'How about you just let me know where I *can't* pitch.'

'It would not be my place to tell you where you *can't* go,' he replied. He was young and stylish, with groomed stubble, a nose-ring, a suit jacket over a logoed orange T-shirt and expensive-looking jeans.

'I just don't want to be getting in anyone's way. You stay here, right?'

'*Stay* is not a word I regularly use.' His answers were becoming evermore evasive, and evermore infuriating with it.

'That tent over there.' I pointed at the green dome he had appeared from. 'Did you sleep in it last night?'

'I did,' he said with a slow smile. I realised I detested him.

'Right. So you stay here. Like I said, I don't want to get in anyone's way. So where do you think would be best for me?'

'How can I say what would be *best* for you?'

For the first time since those cocky students in Bristol, I wanted to punch a man.

'Over there,' I said, gesturing at an empty space near the cathedral wall and surrounded by a pack of eleven tents in neat symmetry. 'Would anyone mind if I put my tent there?'

'It is not for me to say whether...'

I turned my back on him and marched over to the space. Better to pitch up there and get moved on within an hour than spend another second in conversation with that loathsome void of sound bites.

13

I suspected that many of the tents on my 'block' were unoccupied. A picture had recently appeared in the press: a night-time thermal image of the site. It showed that just one in ten of the tents were regularly slept in. Many occupiers pitched up, used their tents as shelter during the day and then returned to their London homes after dark. Other tents, like those around me, seemed to be there purely for show, and remained unused for days on end.

I had but one regular neighbour: Dillon, one of the three homeless men who slept on the square alongside the occupiers. His sleeping bag lay wedged between two close tents, perfectly hidden from all but those who came within a few yards of it. Dillon was short and humble, often seen around the canteen where he was given free meals without question. Everyone was given free meals without question – it was part of the canteen policy – but there were few who took advantage of the opportunity as frequently as Dillon. He had perhaps not been so well fed in years. He drank tea (again free) by the gallon and quelled his nicotine addiction by 'blagging saves' off anyone he saw smoking.

I spent an afternoon in the large white marquee which housed the canteen, helping to serve food and wash pans. The entire back wall was hidden behind stacks of tins, crates of bread and vegetables, industrial-sized bottles of water.

'Where did all this come from?' I asked that day's head chef: an Italian with gleaming whites and an immaculate clean-shave.

'It's all donations,' he replied.

'Donations from who?'

'*Everyone*. Charities, redistribution agencies, supporters, but mostly just people who are passing. We have a lot of support here. A lot of people really care about what we're doing, and they want to help us. Yesterday morning, three guys in suits came in with a huge box of chopped tomatoes. If I'd have seen them on the streets, I would have thought *bankers*. Maybe they were. It didn't matter. They wanted to help us. One said to me: "You can return the favour when it all crashes".' The chef laughed at the memory and swirled a vat of bubbling pasta with a fork. 'Then yesterday afternoon, this old woman – and I mean, in her *nineties* – came in for a cup of tea. I gave her the charm and she loved it. Asked where she could make a donation to the cause. I told her to go to the information tent. She came back five minutes later and said she couldn't find it. Asked if I could pass on the donation for her. She dropped something in my hand so small I could hardly feel it. It was a five-pound note, folded down to the size of a stamp.'

I smiled and thought of my own grandma, who would have done the same. 'She's probably suffering from coalition-cuts more than anyone.'

'Yeah, man. I don't get your government at all. I've been in this country a long time, and the best things about it – healthcare, education, pensions, benefits for the disabled, for the unemployed – they're the things the government seem to stand *against*. It confuses the shit out of me.'

'Is Italy any better?'

'Don't get me started on that shit-hole. Why do you think I'm here?'

Dillon joined the end of the short queue. I piled his plate high with his third lunch serving and said hello to him for the third time. For the third time, I received a nod and nothing more in reply.

'Do you know him?' I asked the chef once Dillon had left the canteen to crouch on the ground outside and shovel the pasta into his mouth.

'Don't recognise him.'

'He's called Dillon. He's homeless, but he sleeps here.'

'Not very talkative, is he? Have you met Pat? He's another homeless guy who lives with us. Complete opposite, though. Can't get him to shut up.'

'I haven't met him. I've heard about him, though. Dillon said there's only three homeless guys who stay here – him, Pat and Doug.'

'Don't know Doug either, but you'll probably see Pat later. He's been away for a few days, but when he's here, he's *here*. He likes to sit at the back and count the stock. Says he's auditing for us and it's important. I know he sneaks a load of food into his bag while he's doing it, and I can't even fucking read the crazy lists he hands to me at the end, but he's a nice guy, and the food's just as much for him as it is for the rest of us.'

He drained the pasta into another cauldron, threw on a litre of tomato and garlic sauce and then gestured at me to bring him more pasta. I rooted through the supplies fit for a military campaign, unearthed a kilo bag of penne and brought it back for the chef, who ripped it open with his hands and upended it into the boiling, cloudy water.

'Why do you think there aren't more homeless sleeping here?' I asked. 'Or at least enjoying the free food? Seems to me that this is the perfect set-up. Space, sustenance, tea, no questions asked, even empty tents.'

'I asked Pat the same thing once. He said the police.'

I grabbed the fork from the table and stirred the hard pasta, hoping he would elaborate. He did.

'There's police all over this place all the time. They're not doing anything, they're not allowed to, but they're always here. Pat said he was scared of the police. But we're not.'

'Perhaps the homeless have more cause for fear than you do.'

'Perhaps,' the chef nodded as he served his hundredth customer that day. 'Perhaps.'

The next evening, Dillon confirmed the chef's hypothesis. He remained wary of me, but our close proximity lent itself to a grudging acceptance of my presence on his part. Plus, I had brought him a fresh cup of tea and, as he sat up in his sleeping bag to grasp it, he perhaps felt the polite need to oblige me while he drank it.

'These kids are looking for a fight,' he said. 'And they'll get it. They keep pushing long enough and they'll get exactly what they want. A night in the cells. Badge of honour. But that's the last thing I need. No such thing as one night in the cells for me.'

'Why would they keep you in for longer?'

'You ask a lot of questions, don't you?'

'I do,' I admitted.

'There's no reason. Doesn't need to be one. They'd find one. I don't trust them. Never have.'

Dillon finished his tea, passed the cup back to me with a quiet thanks, and then pulled the top of the sleeping bag over his head. Our short conversation had come to an end.

I returned to my tent and reflected on Dillon's proclamations. It was highly plausible he had done nothing wrong, had no previous record, but the mere presence of the police fed a paranoia he had been cultivating for years. I had noticed that in many of the rough sleepers I had met: an ingrained distrust of anyone else, from the police to general citizens to other homeless people. It was a survival technique, a tactic of continuation, though it closed the homeless off from those who wanted to help just as much as it protected them from those who intended to harm. In St Mungo's, I had been told that, when you are on the streets, you only have yourself to worry about, and a thousand anxieties of living in the modern world are thereby removed with one stroke. But the knife was double-edged, for when you only have to care for yourself, that lack of care for others can become cancerous, and mutate into anger, then distrust, and ultimately fear. Jeremy Paxman had told me that a bridge of fear existed between the homeless and the non-homeless. I was beginning to see that the bridge had two lanes.

14

I unzipped the tent and held the flap open. Dillon peered cautiously inside. The light of my torch fell upon a single duvet which rested against the back wall, a white bloom of mould edging across its neat tessellations.

'I don't know,' Dillon muttered.

'I haven't seen one person enter or leave this tent in the whole time I've been here.'

'I don't know.'

The rain was thick and brutal, beating an ever-rising crescendo on the tent's roof. Its thunderous clatter had woken me ten minutes before, and I had scampered outside to find Dillon's sleeping bag afloat in a miry puddle. I insisted he sleep in my tent for the night. He refused. I insisted he sleep in someone else's.

'Just use it tonight, at least. It's gone midnight. No one's coming back here until the morning.'

'I don't know.' The rain had plastered his thin hair to his face and the sleeves of his sweatshirt dripped down on to his shoes. I pushed him inside and zipped the door shut behind him.

When I stepped out on to the square at five o'clock in the morning, the rain had stopped, leaving behind a Lake District of pale, stony pools around the tents. Dillon was back outside in his sleeping bag.

The camp was quiet in the mornings. People slowly stirred and began to appear at nine o'clock, spurred into daylight by the cockerel-calls of the garbage-disposal truck and the Italian chef's loud and happy exclamation from the canteen: 'Porridge! I have made *porridge*!' Then the crowds swelled throughout the day as the non-campers joined the ranks for breakfast and another long day of protest. New slogans were scrawled in black pen on to A4 sheets of paper and plastered against any available wall, column or plinth. Posters – some sparse and punchy; others as densely worded as a sermon – came loose and fluttered over the sides of the tents, sticking to clothes-lines and black-tape messages of 'We are the 99%'. Corporate logos were parodied and lampooned between the slogans. On the window of the St Paul's Starbucks, someone had glued a painting of a starving child morphing out of a spilled cup of coffee. Inside, trade was better than ever – there was always at least one anti-capitalism protester in there sipping a latte and taking advantage of the free Wi-Fi.

There was little conversation at the Occupy London site, more just a series of monologues. I enjoyed watching people hold court: the stutters of excitement as they realised others had begun to crowd around them; the inevitable deflation as, one by one, the impromptu audience moved on to the next orator.

I spent a lot of time in my tent. It was peaceful inside, and I knew that the moment I stepped out and joined the throngs I had to be ready to feature in a thousand photos. The press swarmed the campsite at all hours of the day, and most of the occupiers were more than happy to feature in interviews or supply quotes. Cameras, Dictaphones and notepads hovered around every conversation, and the conversations in turn became stilted and contrived, losing their organic flow and substituting it for media-friendly catchphrases. A young and slim girl choreographed the 'Thriller' dance to a score of eager and willing occupiers while a BBC film crew surrounded them. 'We'll take this to the Houses of Parliament!' she screamed, and the dancers moaned in zombie-like agreement. When the cameras disappeared five minutes later, the dancers disbanded, too.

In the afternoons and evenings, a PA system was wheeled out into the middle of the square for the twice-daily General Assemblies. They were strange affairs, filled with speakers whose language was as couched in hedges, adverbs and bureaucratic non-speak as any House of Commons debate. On the afternoon the Dean of St Paul's resigned, I sat on the steps of his former cathedral for the first GA of the day. Some live music was offered as an opener for the session, and a drummer beat his *djembe* while a rapper grabbed the microphone and shouted invectives into it. 'Bank charge, bank charge, what you gonna do?'

It was common at each GA for a spokesperson from each of the site's 'Working Groups' to add a few official sentences to the day's proceedings. Direct Action, Shelter, Outreach and Anonymous UK were all represented, but the site also had its own Media Liaison, and even a bank of individuals who self-policed the site and who were known as the Tranquillity Group. The spokespeople took to the stage, it seemed, to squabble, raising numerous resolutions, objections and counter-resolutions over the microphone. The increasingly disengaged crowd registered their feelings towards each speaker's sentiments with sign language: a waggle of the hands meant approval; a rolling tombola motion meant 'Get on with it'; one raised fist was a clear and imperative 'No' (appellated by the speakers as a 'block'); and a less-certain symbol of disagreement was one's arms crossed in an X across the chest. 'If you don't agree with what our Media Liaison just said,' the compère called out, 'do the X Factor!'

It was customary for the crowd to slowly dissolve as each GA progressed long past its allotted hour. But, on the day of the dean's resignation, a curious incident took place which kept us in our seats throughout.

Though the spokespeople were the only regular orators, anyone was allowed to say a few words over the microphone if they wished. A stout black man in a faux priest costume took to the stage, ignored the proffered microphone, raised his arms into the air and shouted: 'Tent City must go! This is England! If you are white, it will be all right! If you are brown, stick around! If you are black, get to the back! Tent City must go!'

A clamour of occupiers surrounded him, urging him to leave the stage. He refused. 'This is England!' he continued.

'If you are white, it will be all right! If you are brown, stick around! If you are black, get to the back! Tent City must go! This is England! If you are…'

The occupiers formed a circle around him, linked hands and gently kettled him from the stage. He leaned on their arms, beamed and persisted with his chant.

'If you are white…'

The Outreach spokesman, quiet and prone to nervous laughter, took the microphone. 'We've just been informed that this man is a street-performer. He's been recognised from Covent Garden. This is just a silly act.'

'If you are brown…'

'He's been paid to sabotage the GA!' a man shouted from the audience.

'If you are black…'

'The best thing we can do,' the Outreach spokesman continued, 'is just ignore him and carry on with the things we need to talk about.'

He did his best, the PA was turned up, but the man shouted louder, and all became lost in the cacophony.

'This is England! Tent City must go!'

An irate young woman in a trench coat launched herself on to the stage and ripped the microphone from the spokesman's ineffectual hands. 'This man is deliberately trying to thwart us!' she screamed while feedback howled from the lone speaker. 'Ignore him! Don't give him any attention! We must not let anyone disrupt our order here!'

The crowd fell silent for a moment, and the man timed his retort perfectly. 'Are you trying,' he bellowed, 'to *evict* me?'

The crowd dissolved into laughter, the farcical hilarity of it all suddenly evident, and the GA came to an end.

15

The site slowly cleared in the hours between the closing of the evening GA and the closing of the Underground. After only a few days at St Paul's, I came to believe the veracity of those thermal images which showed only 10 per cent of the tents occupied at night. By midnight, an eerie silence settled over the site.

Nevertheless, those hardcore who stayed were beginning to wear each other out. Tempers frayed at two in the morning. Alcohol and drugs were strictly prohibited on the site, but we all knew they were consumed illicitly. Each night, at least one fiery and inebriated shouting-match was launched over the heads of the tents. Perhaps someone was still playing a guitar, perhaps a couple's sex had become ludicrous in its volume, perhaps late-night revellers fresh from a nightclub kick-out had sauntered past the cathedral looking for a fight. Either way, anger and noise rose and rose each night until a member of the Tranquillity Group appeared, frustrated and sleep-deprived, to quell whatever needless disturbance was building. These tranquillity folk were, I began to realise, good people, intent on keeping peace, even if it was four o'clock in the morning. And their objective was always met, and always done so through their calm and pragmatic subjugations. Except, of course, for the night before I left.

16

I had made few friends at St Paul's, and this depressed me. It was probably my fault: it all seemed rather irrelevant to me. These people were fighting a worthy cause in a noble manner, but their issues diverged from mine. I wanted to know how a tramp might fare in the twenty-first century, what the causes and the effects and the experiences of a rough sleeper today might be and, except for Pat and Doug (who I never met – rumour had it that they had left) and Dillon (who rarely spoke to me), my neighbours were not homeless. They were only houseless temporarily. They were, dare I say it, like me – this living-on-the-streets thing was born out of choice rather than necessity – and I had little interest in meeting more people like me, for that was not the aim of my journey.

I found myself missing Ian, Diana and Marek, and decided to walk to Parliament Square one day to see them. I did not want to meet Greg, hoped he would be out for the afternoon, but the thought of Ian's raucous laughter, of Marek's shy smile and of Diana's kindness negated any threat Greg might present.

I arrived to find half the number of tents, and only Diana amongst them. A man who wasn't Greg appeared from her tent and stood beside her possessively as she gave me a hug. I explained my reasons for leaving, recounting the story of the policeman and his threat of arrest.

'You did the right thing,' Diana said. 'Don't get arrested. That's stupid. Some of the boys were suspicious that morning, though. Greg thought you were a spy.'

'Greg always thought I was a spy. It's one of the reasons I was happy to leave. Greg made me feel pretty uncomfortable here.' I noticed Diana's new companion bristle each time I mentioned Greg's name.

'It's why I'm off, as well,' Diana said. 'Not Greg. He disappeared. Didn't like living in a tent, in one place in full view of everyone.' She pointed over to the police officers at the gates to the Houses of Parliament. 'But it's been getting worse and worse here.'

I could see that. Six riot vans were parked around the square, each full to capacity with reclining police officers. The night before, a mob of drunken revellers had surrounded the tents and chanted threats. The security wardens had called the police, who had appeared within minutes and dispersed the crowd. I remembered the security warden I met on my first morning, who asked me: 'Have you ever considered that we might be here for *your* protection?'

We sat inside Diana's tent while she brewed cups of tea. Perhaps understanding that I was not there to steal his woman, Diana's companion, Paul, had warmed to me and had begun to explain his personal five-year plan.

'All I care about's me son. She's all right to him, but that prick of a boyfriend, he's a shit. I need to get him out of there. But the first thing they tell you is "you need an address". Without that, they can't do shit.'

'We're on the same page, Charlie,' Diana said, pulling the kettle from the gas-burner and decanting it into three dirty cups. 'I told you about my court case, didn't I?'

'Actually,' I said, taking the warm cup from her hands. 'You never really explained it to me.'

'Didn't she? All she ever talks about to me!'

'Leave it, Paul.' Diana slapped him playfully on the arm. 'It's my daughter, see? She was in a care-home for a while, and she used to come visit me when she was allowed. But she got physically abused when she was there. Multiple head-wounds. I *know* it happened while she was in care, but they're saying I did it when she came to visit. But I couldn't do that. You believe me, don't you, Charlie?'

I did.

'So I'm getting the same problems as Paul. No one will take me seriously and take my side unless, and they all say the same thing, unless I've got an address. But we've just got some good luck. We managed to get a static caravan just outside London, got its own postcode and everything, and now I can get her back legitimately.'

Diana pronounced that last word with relish, and I got the sense that she was excited at the prospect of plugging back into the grid.

'So we're off tomorrow,' she continued. 'And it couldn't come at a better time. Things haven't been good here. You were right to leave when you did.'

'Maybe,' I said, 'but I've missed it here. I've been over at St Paul's with the Occupy London lot.'

An uncomfortable silence fell, both pairs of eyes dropped from mine, and we all drank tea awkwardly.

'We don't like them,' Paul finally said.

'Why not?'

'They've got them politicians working at all hours to try and find a way to evict people who put up a tent in London. They'll pass a law to get them out. And when they do, they'll use the same law on us here.'

I sensed severe disapproval, something akin to the kind I used to feel from Greg. Diana, as always, diffused the mounting tension.

'That doesn't matter to us any more, though, does it, Paul? We've got our caravan.'

'True,' Paul muttered, slurping on his tea.

'Fact is, I can't wait to see the back of this place,' Diana continued. 'A lot's happened since you've been gone, Charlie.'

A lot had, and she enumerated it in detail. The same day I left, a man moved on to my pitch and erected his tent. Soon after, everyone began to notice that things were going missing from their own tents. They confronted the man, who admitted to his thieving, and then, as one, they repossessed his tent and kicked him out. He had returned two nights later, early in the evening, and a nasty fight had broken out.

'We got rid of him, but that's happening more and more often these days.'

'Some twat started on me the other day,' Paul agreed. 'I nutted him.'

'Paul,' Diana remonstrated. 'But he's right. It's getting too violent here. People don't trust each other any more.'

'It's because of those two pricks,' Paul said.

Diana nodded. 'You met them, didn't you, Charlie?' She described the young couple, Rolly and Rudy, who begged each day and then flashed their notes around the campsite at night: Rolly with his diabetics-paunch and leather jacket; Rudy with her contrived lingo and jittery knees.

'It was this huge scandal,' Diana said. 'The police came in one afternoon and abducted her. It was good for Rolly that he was still begging and she'd come back on her own. The police came back later that evening looking for him. Turns out Rudy's lied to us all, even to him. Said she was eighteen, but she was only fifteen. Ran away from her foster home. Told Rolly she'd been on the streets for three years, but it was only a month before she met him. The police said if he came back we should let them know. Said they wanted him for questioning. Paedophilia, like. But he didn't have a clue. When he got back, we told him what had happened and he just did one. Haven't seen him since.'

'Where's Ian?' I asked, gesturing over at the still-standing Rainbow Tent. 'Unusual for him to not be on guard duty.'

Diana shook her head sadly. 'He's in jail. I think.'

Ian, Diana explained, had started spending more and more time at his girlfriend's flat. He had also, for reasons Diana could not fathom, started to carry a knife. One evening, at his girlfriend's for dinner, he had produced the knife and threatened to stab the two male friends eating with them. The police were called, Ian created a scene, and he was arrested and taken away. The girlfriend had come to the square the next day looking for him, but he had not been back since.

'He was getting wilder each day,' Diana said. 'Drinking in the mornings, trying to pick fights with tourists. He started to scare me. He had a lot of problems.'

There was ice in my stomach. I lamented what had happened to Ian, more so because it was deeply plausible. 'What about Marek?'

'Now *he's* done good for himself,' Diana replied, and my spirits lifted. 'He got accepted into a shelter. A group of nuns run it. They're really strict on him – he's got a curfew and has to work all day either in the building or handing out donations to other shelters and refuges. But he loves it. He comes by some afternoons and drops off coffee and bread for us. I've never seen him look so happy. He says the nuns treat him like a ten-year-old nephew, but he's earning the roof over his head, and they've sorted out medicine for him so that he can sort his leg out and get back into work. It's all he wants, all he talks about. Work, work, work.'

'He's a good bloke, that one,' Paul affirmed.

I revelled in the good news after all the horror stories of arrests, runaways, thieving, knives and betrayal. And I liked Diana's closing repetition. Marek wanted to work, and that was key. He would, I had no doubt, do so, and this was the best way for him to get back on his feet, as lamed as one of them was.

I stood up and thanked them both for the tea and the conversation. 'Good luck with your daughter,' I told Diana, and to Paul: 'Good luck with your son.'

'And good luck with your book,' Diana said.

'You're writing a book?' Paul asked.

I nodded.

'Make sure you tell the truth, mate,' he said.

'I will,' I promised.

17

Feti and I sat on the steps of St Paul's Cathedral while the evening's General Assembly droned on. Between us lay a plastic carrier bag filled with cans of cheap ale, and we took turns sharing them out into concealed plastic cups.

'I love this!' Feti cried, lighting a roll-up and toking hard. '*This*...' he pointed at the current speaker, one of the Media Liaison team, who was proudly detailing her conversation with a *Guardian* journalist, '... *this* is why I want to become British national. *This* is important!'

'Why?'

'*Why*? You ask me *why*? Look at all this. You think this can happen in many other countries?'

'From what I've read in the papers, it seems to be.'

'Yeah, yeah. In Western countries. The developed world. The First World. But I tell you, you try to do this in *my* country, in fucking *Algeria*, and it all over, man. But here you can *protest*. You understand how important that is? You should be proud. A man has to have principles, you know? It is why I came here, to Britain. Men can stand up for their principles here, not like in Algeria. I swum the *Channel* to get here.'

'Piss off!'

'Yes! I did! It is true! No lie! They caught me in the *sea*!' I had visions of police boats, of a huge fishing rod, of Feti dangling gleefully from the end of it. 'I had to wait six days in prison while they threaten to deport me. People gave me cigarettes – not tobacco, *real* cigarettes – so that I would tell them my story of swimming the Channel. I smoked like a *king*.'

Feti seemed to enjoy protest for the sake of protest. Perhaps his fundamental principle was a defence of the right to defend one's principles.

'I went on the student riots earlier this year. I was *kettled*, man!'

'Are you a student?'

'No. I'm a gardener. But I was there anyway. They kettled me all day. Nowhere to go! So I made a fire to keep warm.'

With plenty of tinned ale in my belly, I fell asleep quickly that night, woken a few hours later by the reverberating thump of something bouncing off the exterior of my tent in concert with a male scream.

'I'm gonna fucking *kill* you!' The voice ricocheted off the cathedral and echoed across the site.

I unzipped the door and poked my head out of the tent. The rapid dip and rise of a torch flashed across the square as a young man raced forward in search of the disturbance. I recognised him as the spokesperson for the Tranquillity Group. His light found its target: two men grappling on the floor, a tangle of legs and shoulders. Muffled expletives accompanied the unmistakeable noise of flesh hitting flesh. Somehow, inexplicable in the torchlight, a shoe cascaded through the air. A woman clad in thin pyjamas howled inaudible invectives from the ringside. Other heads began to appear from other tents. Some laughed; others barked 'Break it up!' and 'We're trying to sleep!'; one wept and moaned like a Spanish grandmother at a funeral. The Tranquillity Group spokesman reached into the scuffle and found his leverage, splitting the two brawlers with a scissor-like motion of his arms. Other men had walked over and grabbed the two fighters, pulling them away from each other. They continued to kick and paw, ineffectual bursts of machismo reduced to comic bravado.

'You need your fucking *head* looking at!'

'I'm gonna wait for you, cunt!'

'Slash your fucking *throat*!'

I slipped back into my tent as others appeared from theirs and sauntered over to the growing group. *Wait for it*, I thought, *someone's going to say...*

The expected proclamation came with unerring timing. 'Guys!' the voice bellowed. 'We shouldn't be fighting each other! We should be fighting *them*!'

My prediction of cheesy movie sound bites gave me no solace that night. The argument raged until the sun rose.

An emergency General Assembly was called the following morning. Reports of the incident conflicted and contradicted. The two guys got drunk and had a little scuffle. The two guys got drunk and beat the shit out of each other. The two guys got drunk and one of them sexually harassed a girl. The two guys got drunk and one of them called the other a nigger. Whatever had actually happened, I gathered it was because the two guys got drunk.

What troubled the GA speakers most of all, however, was that the two guys were occupiers. They were not visitors, not drunken clubbers on their way home, not even day-supporters, but men who lived and slept on the square every day and night. They had been evicted, of course, but how to stop it all happening again? We all, it was explained, lived in such close proximity, and aggression was bound to result. This was the worst flare-up, but it was not the first. The Tranquillity Group were exhausted. The Media Group wondered what the press would make of it. Outreach said we had lost our bearings. Anonymous UK said that it was all a natural reaction to our circumstances. The spokespeople held the stage for the next two hours, squabbling over possible outcomes, venting hypotheses and semantic quandaries. A

'20 Point Peace Plan' was disseminated and then quibbled over, criterion by criterion. Few listened.

18

Whatever had happened and whatever was going to happen as a result of the night's disturbance, camaraderie had become displaced on the campsite, and people eyed each other with a newfound distrust. Eviction rumours had always abounded at St Paul's, it was part of the daily conversation. 'Tonight's the night,' people whispered to each other. 'They're coming.' But that day those rumours seemed heightened. It was true that the police presence had doubled in Paternoster Square throughout the day, and there were more riot vans and marked cars parked up on the kerbsides than I had ever seen before. Perhaps people were attempting to supplant the previous night's fight by projecting their distrust outwards, but it could not be denied that we were being watched by more and more eyes every hour. 'Are you ready for it?' I was asked more than once, fathoming in the words of the questioners an excitement I did not like.

After lunch, I walked back to my tent. Dillon had rolled up his sleeping bag and was shouldering his rucksack.

'Are you off?' I asked.

'Fucking right. It was good while it lasted, but I can't be doing with the police. I'm not getting arrested tonight.'

I found myself agreeing with him.

It took fifteen minutes to pack my knapsack, to fold down and re-sheath my tent. A few watched me as I worked, but only one approached. It was the infuriating equivocator I had met on my arrival.

'Why are you leaving?' he asked.

'*Leave* is a strong word,' I replied. 'Is it your place to ask me such things?'

He smiled at me, and it irritated me that I had not irritated him.

'We're getting evicted tonight. And it'll be forceful.' When he spoke the last word, he smiled. I looked into his eyes and knew immediately that he looked forward to it. He couldn't wait to test his mettle against the police; he relished the opportunity to get righteous and angry. Deep down, everyone here wanted to get righteous and angry.

'I'm finding it hard to share your enthusiasm,' I said. 'I'm with Dillon on this one. I don't want to get arrested. Maybe that makes me a coward.'

He nodded, confirming my suspicion.

'You know,' I said, 'there's people here doing good and important things, working tirelessly to raise awareness of issues which need to be addressed. But tell me, what have you actually done? All I've ever seen you do is sit around, drinking coffee and talking shit.'

He gestured at the placard in his hand, the same one he had carried when I first met him. THIS IS NOT A PROTEST. THIS IS A RIGHT.

'Exactly,' I said. 'That's your contribution. A banal aphorism.'

'Fuck you,' came his reply, still with a smile.

'And that's why I'm not sticking around.' I lifted my tent and knapsack from the ground, one in each hand, and left St Paul's. It was time to go home.

I used Marcus's Oyster Card (I could return it to him later, along with his tent) to catch a Number 11 bus from St Paul's to Victoria. Arcing through Westminster, we passed Parliament Square at a crawl. I noticed an empty space where Diana's tent had been. Perhaps this was fortunate, for every other tent had been cordoned off behind strict fencing, and police officers stood at two-metre intervals around the campsite. Protesters and homeless alike, more than I had ever seen at one time on the square, harried the police with heated discussions. Guilt at my desertion mingled with relief to have made the decision to leave it all behind. A single wish rose above it all: that the coming winter would not be too cold.

My eyelids grew heavy as the bus stalled in traffic along Victoria Street. The shouts and arguments and noise which succeeded the fight outside St Paul's had left me bereft of sleep for the rest of the night. As I thought of it, I remembered my first night on Gwithian's sand dunes. My journey had circled back upon itself. Those two nights were so alike: they were both cold and uncomfortable, they both gave birth to little respite, and they had both left me utterly miserable.

As the bus crawled nearer to the coach station, I found myself reflecting on all the outdoor nights of my journey. Sleeping rough was, I decided with little originality, far more extreme and difficult than anything I had ever done before: a descent into a lifestyle which was still, after all these months, alien to me, for I could not conceive how anyone could cope with it. And sleeping rough on city streets was the bottom rung. I would not wish it on anyone. Those dunes and fields, those woods and cliff-tops, they had been tolerable; but those nights on the streets of London, even the ones I weathered within the shelter of a tent, had left me feeling more vulnerable and threatened and exposed and imperilled and insecure than any other place I had visited in the world.

When you spend time on the streets, you learn how terrifying other people can be. Whether in cars or on foot, whether they were my neighbours or passers-by, the sheer volume of people had been inescapable. How long must it take a tramp to get used to footsteps? How low does one have to get before one's worries of violence are finally replaced by indifference? If I really wanted to become a tramp I would have to get there, to that place where one can curl up anywhere in the world in any weather and relinquish consciousness. To reach such a state would take years, I supposed, perhaps decades. It requires a dedication I do not have; a dedication most rough sleepers only discover out of needful obligation. For all my posturing, for all my immersion and deprivation, I never truly became a tramp. I just bit at the heels of the lifestyle. Even when I was most down and out, I always had something others did not: I had a home, and it was ready for my return whenever I felt the need.

My final night in Tent City triggered that need. I was tired, I stank, I hated my two T-shirts, despised the weight of my knapsack, and my beard looked more ridiculous than ever. I disembarked the bus at Victoria Station and sat on a bench, munching on a cereal bar and holding on to the peak of my cap with my other hand lest the heightening wind rip it from my head. I had started this journey with a question: what was it like to be a tramp in the twenty-first century? There, on that bench, the answer resounded in a few simple words. It was abominable. Surely, it always had been. Even for those who chose the lifestyle in the past, perhaps only a few had managed to make a living, had succeeded in finding safe places to sleep night after night. And they, that lucky minority, would have still forged an existence far from the cheery and mythical tramps one meets in folklore and fairytales. Perhaps that was why there were so few tramps left. Who would choose this?

Taking the last of my cash from my pocket, I walked into the coach station and bought a ticket for the next bus home. Back there was a bed with a duvet, central heating, television, a long couch, a loving cat, fresh food in the fridge, an oven to cook it in, electric light, clocks, a wardrobe of clothes, two machines to wash and then dry them in, wine, shelves of books, a shower, my computer, my music and, most importantly, my wife.

Inside the coach as it idled within Victoria Station's confines, I lazily fingered the wedding ring I had kept on my finger. I had had an internal debate about it, I remembered, at the beginning of the journey. I had divested myself of anything which could be stolen from me on the road, and for a long while I had considered leaving my wedding ring at home along with my credit cards and iPod and non-charity-shop clothes. But I had been unable to remove the ring, the symbol of my marriage. And, while I thought about it, I realised that no one had even noticed it. I felt pleased about that, as pleased as I was when the engine stirred and the coach moved out and away from the streets.

CHAPTER NINE

THE END

I

At 7.30 p.m. on Monday 16 January 2012, police vans appeared at Parliament Square to evict the protesters and homeless who lived there. Under the Police Reform and Social Responsibility Act, they legitimately removed all tents and sleeping equipment from the area. Two people were arrested and some of the homeless were referred to hostels, but most fled back to the anonymity of the streets. By sunrise the following morning, Parliament Square was cleared for the first time in a decade.

Exactly six weeks later, on Monday 27 February 2012, following a High Court decision to evict the Occupy London campaign, a regiment of police officers and bailiffs entered the square outside St Paul's Cathedral at midnight and began to clear the site, loading tents into the back of a garbage truck. Twenty arrests were made after a barricade was built from pallets and wooden shelving. I feel certain I know who some of the resisters were, and hope their night in the cells passed without incident.

In the Easter holidays of April 2012, I retraced my route, though this time at the wheel of my VW Camper van. The new journey took a tenth of the time and cost ten times as much.

I found Jan on the same bench at Broad Quay in Bristol where we met the first time. We walked to The Wild Goose together and ate beans on toast. 'I am a salesman,' Jan said, pointing to the sack of *Big Issues* below the table. 'And I will be for a long time.'

Sue was likewise at her post. The man she had lived with had kicked her out, but she would not tell me why. She had been back on the streets for the last two months.

I asked both, and a few others, about Stan. None had heard of him.

I spent a day walking Bradford-on-Avon and its outskirts in search of Nigel, but could not find him.

In London, at Frank's regular pitch in Covent Garden, a new *Big Issue* seller had taken over the location. 'Frank?' he said. 'Not been here for months. He works at Sainsbury's now.'

On the Strand, I met a man who knew Diana. 'Shacked up in a caravan somewhere,' he said.

I called all the hostels in Central London: some had Mareks in residence, but none fitted my description, and I did not know his surname.

Passing Victoria Square, I thought I saw Greg stood in a group of six before a three-foot-high pile of duvets and bags. I did not venture over.

I contacted my liaison at St Mungo's and asked if she or anyone she knew had heard of Ian and could tell me where he might be, whether on the streets or in jail, but she had no clue, and nor did any of the rough sleepers I asked across the capital.

On the drive back to my Cornish home, I stopped one final time in Bristol, determined to locate Stan. I visited all our old spots – Castle Park at three o'clock in the afternoon, the Methodist chapel, The Wild Goose – but I never saw him. Finally, I happened upon the man Stan bought his cheap tobacco from. He had last seen Stan a few days before that winter's snowstorms, and that was months ago. I remembered the way Stan sometimes passed out into a vodka-coma before he was able to get himself back to his garage, and found myself dearly hoping that he had simply left Bristol for the next stop on his tramping odyssey.

2

Back in Cornwall, I found work teaching again, and began to regularly play a game with my Year 11s in the few weeks remaining before their GCSEs. Based on Radio 4's *Just a Minute*, and stolen as a teaching technique from my own English teacher, the game required students, picked at random, to speak for sixty seconds on a subject of my choice without hesitation or repetition. The Year 11s groaned each time I interrupted normal proceedings for a bout of the game, but I always explained that it would help them think and respond spontaneously, something necessary in exams, and they would grudgingly acquiesce. Not long after the Easter holidays, I picked on Tom, and bid him stand up.

'Tom,' I intoned in the mock-serious broadcaster's voice I had come to enjoy. 'You need to speak for sixty seconds without hesitation or repetition on the subject of... the homeless.'

Tom launched into his impromptu speech. 'The homeless are people without homes. They live on the streets and beg for money. Other names for them are hobos, gyppos or pikeys. They have dogs and sell *The Big Issue*. They don't work and our taxes pay for them. We call James homeless...' a nod at his best friend James, followed by a collective snigger from the rest of the class '... because he once ate a kebab off the floor. The homeless have nothing and...' a pause, but too brief to be called '... and they have nothing because they do nothing... the homeless are...'

This pause was long enough to be a bona fide hesitation, and Tom's friends shouted it before I could. Tom sat down.

For a brief moment, I considered telling Tom and the rest of the class about my journey, about the homeless I had met, about the tramp I had been. But the thought dissolved less than a second after it had formed. I knew too well what the responses would be, and the respect I would lose.

Later that evening, I contemplated my decision to keep quiet about my experience. It was a matter of shame. My students thought of the homeless in the same way many adults across the country think. The homeless, to them, were scum, and if they ever suspected that their teacher – their guide through the most important exams of their lives so far – had been homeless, then the shame would have rebounded about the classroom's walls.

Not that I had, I realised, even really been homeless. My experiences on the streets from Cornwall to London had in no way been representative of all the homeless across England. I thought about my first book, which I had hoped would encapsulate the experiences of teachers in the country's most difficult schools, delve into why they were leaving in droves, and then provide answers.

Within this book, I have not employed the same tactics. This is not a dialectic nor a polemic, not an answer to the riddle of homelessness nor an explanation of why or how it occurs. This is, instead, the story of my own journey from Cornwall to London; my 300-mile tramp of footsore days and rough nights followed by my brief life on London's streets; my choice. And, living with and amongst the homeless, sharing vodka and beer and stories with them, speaking to them and a number of others who have forged noble careers out of aiding and assisting rough sleepers, I gained at least a rare insight into the kind of street life I never before knew.

If I have managed to successfully share that insight with you and, perhaps, along the way given voice to a few real, dispossessed and disenfranchised people who continue to exist in your world, and who continue to be ignored by most mainstream literature and media, then I can derive satisfaction from that. And I hope that, maybe, it might alter your perception, even slightly, when you next walk your local streets, when you next pass a rough sleeper – I hope that, maybe, you might offer them some money, or just some companionship. A conversation, or at least a smile. They will be able to tell you far better than I can what it is truly like to be a homeless person in the UK today. They have opened my eyes, and for that I am grateful for my brief life as a twenty-first century tramp.

ACKNOWLEDGEMENTS

There are many I met on the streets who I express heartfelt thanks to, and many I do not. I hope the reader will divine from my words which camp each individual falls into.

To extol the virtues of the myriad institutions and organisations which exist to aid rough sleepers in twenty-first-century England would require a whole book in itself, and so I will enumerate just those I happened upon along my own short journey – in particular, The Wild Goose in Bristol, St Mungo's in Camden, Anchor House in Newham, and the One Percent Scheme in Hackney. All are doing invaluable work, and demand the reader's attention.

Thanks also must go to those who have offered me financial support over the year it has taken me to write up my journey. The K Blundell Trust awarded me a bounteous sum with which I was able to fight off work for two whole months and dedicate myself to this text. Their generosity was as well received as it was unanticipated, and without their help this book would have taken me perhaps six months longer to finish.

For similar reasons, the details of which I will not go into, I must have it in print that, without the altruism and philanthropy of Adrian Cox, the means to write every day would have diminished to a pinhole speck.

I am extremely grateful for the advice, suggestions and encouragement of those at Summersdale who have worked with me to polish and mould this book into the best and shiniest shape I am capable of, whose constructive criticism was always spot-on, and whose kind words and heartening sentiments matched the privilege I feel at having the opportunity to work with them. They are Jennifer Barclay, Abbie Headon, Stephen Brownlee, Alastair Williams and Ray Hamilton.

It goes without saying, but I'll say it anyway, that Michelle, Mary, Jodi, Kel, Barrie, Josh, Debbie, Alistair, Aaron, Kellie, Ian, Sam, Ben, Jess, Marcus, Rachel, Jo, Bryn, Dave, Amy, Tim, Cassie, Allan, Jake, Bertie and Digby were there throughout with differing levels of support: support which I needed as I walked from Cornwall to London in late 2011, a twenty-first century tramp with no fixed abode.

EXTREME
SLEEPS

ADVENTURES OF A WILD CAMPER

PHOEBE SMITH

EXTREME SLEEPS

Adventures of a Wild Camper

Phoebe Smith

£8.99

Paperback

ISBN: 978-1-84953-393-5

Veteran globetrotter Phoebe Smith sets out to prove that outdoor adventures are available in the UK which rival anything found elsewhere in the world. In this sometimes scary, frequently funny and intriguing journey around the country, Phoebe attempts to discover and conquer its wildest places.

From spending the night in the decaying wreckage of a World War Two bomber at Bleaklow to pitching next to the adrenaline-inducing sheer drops of Lizard Point, Phoebe's extreme sleeps defy her perceptions of the great outdoors and teach her about herself along the way.

'A wonderful, wild collection of tales that will either inspire you to grab your sleeping bag and head for the door, or book a suite at the Ritz!'
Kate Humble

'small boat, great read'
Tom Cunliffe

CIRCLE LINE

AROUND LONDON IN A SMALL BOAT

Steffan Meyric Hughes

CIRCLE LINE

Around London in a Small Boat

Steffan Meyric Hughes

£8.99

Paperback

ISBN: 978-1-84953-293-8

Magic, to a sailor, is harnessing the wind – getting something for nothing – the surprise of a gust, the boon of a side-wind and the trial of a headwind and best of all, the moment when a change in direction means turning away from the head seas and wind and running down the wind in a new warm silence.

In 1969, man flew to the moon and sailed around the world solo. In 2009, sailor and Londoner Steffan Meyric Hughes thought he'd try something a little closer to home, becoming the first to sail and row around London in a small boat. Along the way, he discovers the truth behind boats, the sea and rivers, the history of the great city's future and great secrets of the mysterious Thames: wrecks, bombs and intrigue. *Circle Line* is the story of a unique journey on the forgotten waterways of one of the world's greatest capitals; an investigation into the way we live today; and a humorous, sometimes moving trip down memory lane.

Have you enjoyed this book?
If so, why not write a review on your favourite website?

If you're interested in finding out more about our books,
find us on Facebook at **Summersdale Publishers** and
follow us on Twitter at **@Summersdale**.

Thanks very much for buying this Summersdale book.

www.summersdale.com